STORIES *of* MUSIC

Volume 1

Stories of Music: Volume 1 - published in 2015
Published by Timbre Press LLC
ISBN: 978-0-9969327-0-7 (pbk)
ISBN: 978-0-9969327-1-4 (companion web edition)

Cover design by Dejan Mijailovic
Typesetting / interior design by Holly E. Tripp
Compiled and edited by Holly E. Tripp
Printed by IngramSpark

Timbre Press LLC, P.O. Box 201435, Denver, CO 80220, www.timbrepress.com.

Printed on acid-free paper.

10 9 8 7 6 5 4 3 2 1

STORIES of MUSIC

Volume 1

Edited by

Holly E. Tripp

Foreword by
Dan Cohen

timbre
press

"Without music,
life would be a mistake."

- Friedrich Nietzsche

Contents

Suggestions for Enjoyment of This Book

Stories of Music is a multimedia book, and the stories that follow sometimes include audio or video components. These components can be accessed by using QR codes and simple URLs provided throughout the book that will direct you to the companion web edition (supported by all modern browsers). So that readers have easy access to the web edition, it is free and open to anyone. For this reason, it only includes the digital content and a couple other select works from the print book (for previewing purposes). Print readers have access to all of the stories.

Using QR Codes

It is recommended that you download a QR code reader app for your mobile device if you do not already have one (search for "QR code" in your app store and you will find there are several that are free to download). QR codes are provided for stories that include audio or video. Using your QR code reader, simply hold your mobile device over a QR code within the book. Once the code is scanned, you will be directed to the same page within the web edition, where the multimedia work can be played.

Using Simple URLs

If you choose not to use QR codes to access the audio and video content, you will also find simple URLs that you can manually type into your browser (on your mobile device or computer). These will also direct you to the same page within the web edition where the multimedia work can be played.

Navigating the Companion Web Edition for the Best Experience

The user experience within the companion web edition was designed to be very intuitive. From your mobile device, you can simply swipe, or tap on the arrows at either side of your screen, to flip through the pages. You can also pinch to zoom in and out. On mobile devices, it is better to use the landscape position for the best viewing of photographs. This keeps photo spreads (where a photo takes up two pages) from being cut off. Also, because audio and video pieces only play within their individual pages, the landscape view allows you to see two pages while playing these works, so you can enjoy more of the story at once.

For the same reasons as listed above, it is recommended that readers who access the web edition with their computers also use the spread view; see the web edition menu items on the top-left of any page, and then click on "single-page mode" to turn the single-page view on or off (look for the icon that looks like an open book).

Foreword

We are all our own experts on music. Yet, as rich as our musical experience might be, perhaps we are less curious about, or rather, more unaware of what others are experiencing. We might think, *what more is there to know?*

A specific song can bring to mind memories and feelings of experiences long past. Spending time with music we love can help us manage our moods, speed the passage of time, and help us engage with the world around us. Watching someone with Alzheimer's light up when reconnected with music they love from their youth is at the core of our effort at the nonprofit Music & Memory.

Ask ten people to talk about how music has impacted their lives and you'll get ten different stories. Music is a global phenomenon. It is integral to all cultures and religions. Rhythm is built into our DNA, perhaps developed over eons.

But rarely do we learn just how rich the tapestry of others' personal musical voyages might be.

Holly Tripp provides a public service by probing our collective consciousness and shining a light on many of these powerful stories. More than 1,000 submissions flooded her inbox, from which she has selected the most intriguing, the most artful, and the most surprising.

I'm certain you will find the stories herein satisfying, as each selection reveals the powerful connection we all have to music. The more we understand how each of us is affected by music, the better we will be at using it in creative and inspiring ways.

Dan Cohen, MSW
Founder and Executive Director, Music & Memory
New York, New York

Preface

In 1980, my great grandmother, Florence Gwendolyn Fuller Rasco, sat down to write her autobiography, *From Alpha to Omega or From Scratch to Now*. Aged 86 at the time, she shared stories of significant life events, as one would imagine, but also brief accounts that documented her family's way of life in rural Missouri—some that were most unexpected and charming. One such story painted a picture of a young Gwendolyn (the name she went by) dancing to the music of fiddle players who, when the weather was bad, would share their music through a telephone party line:

> *We kids would all play in another room from the grownups. Unbeknown to anyone, my uncle Bill Ellis had taught me to tap dance. So, one night when the music was really good for dancing, my feet just would not stay put. I was dancing, and the other kids were laughing and clapping. Someone came to the door to see what all the noise was about. So, I had to go in and dance for everyone!*

> *Sometimes when the weather was too bad to get out, the fiddlers would give the [party] line ring and everyone would take down the receivers and they would play so we could all hear.*

When I first read this account several years ago, it occurred to me how fascinating our individual experiences with music can be. I never would have imagined such a story, and it stuck with me. Interestingly, my grandmother went to work for the phone company in the 1940s, and she worked there for many years.

In the home where I grew up, in Kansas City, music was all around me. Both of my parents played guitar and would sing to my siblings and me—"Danny's Song" by Loggins & Messina was a family favorite. They encouraged us in music—to play music ourselves, to appreciate the art, and to do something with it. I was always surprised they never thought they were talented enough to do much with it themselves, but I tried to make them proud: I was active in school choir, played clarinet and piano, and I took up guitar, as well, when I was a teenager. I also took an interest in songwriting; it began with writing silly songs with my brother Brandon—we fancied ourselves comedians as well—and I still write music today (more serious songs now), more than twenty years later.

January 9, 2008, we lost Brandon to a fatal car accident, just two days before his thirty-fifth birthday. Everyone who had known him was devastated . . . I couldn't comprehend it. It was only through music, which bonded Brandon and me, that I was finally able to come to terms with his death. The tragic event seemed to ignite my songwriting, and I wrote nearly twenty songs that year (that's a lot for me). The songs would come to me in my sleep, when I would dream of being with him again or even getting the chance to say goodbye. I kept a photo of my brother front and center in my creative space; it felt like we were together again. His picture remains on my office desk as I write this now, and I hold in my mind the proud look on his face when I sang to him for what would be the last time.

These are just a few of the touching and poignant experiences I have had with music, which inspired the idea for this book. I know my stories are among countless tales that people all around the world have. While I cherish how music has moved *me* over the years, and I could likely fill a book with my stories alone, I am endlessly curious about how music impacts other people—from cultural traditions, travel experiences, and musicianship to healing, historical accounts, and music's place in our relationships with others. *Stories of Music* was born from this curiosity. This collection is an opportunity to explore the various musical experiences people have had, to create a community around music storytelling, and to celebrate the feelings music can instill within us.

Music plays an important role in our lives, which is why in addition to compiling these stories to share, I'm also donating a portion of the proceeds from the sale of this book to give back to organizations whose work is centered on bringing music into the lives of others. Hungry for Music has impacted thousands of children globally in its twenty-one-year history, acquiring and donating instruments to those who are hungry to learn how to play. MUSIC & MEMORY[SM], which brings personalized music into the lives of the elderly or infirm through digital music technology, is vastly improving the quality of life for people struggling with Alzheimer's, dementia, and other cognitive and physical challenges. These organizations continue to grow their impact, and they are an inspiration for changing lives through music.

It is my hope that readers will enjoy the distinctive works and genres offered in *Stories of Music*. I also hope this anthology, as well as the efforts of Hungry for Music and Music & Memory, will evoke more stories . . . and that I will have the opportunity to hear them.

Holly E. Tripp
November 2015

Introduction

Music is something we all have in common. It transcends religion, race, language, and even time. It fuels our emotions, our creativity, and how we experience the world around us. This universal nature of music is what I hoped to capture in this anthology—stories we can all relate to. I invited authors and artists from around the globe to share their stories of music, and to do so in the medium and genre of their choice—to tell their stories their way—as long as the stories were true.

When I first put out the call for submissions for *Stories of Music*, I thought I might get fifty stories, 100 if I were really lucky. As the submission period went on, and people learned about the project, I was blown away to have collected more than 1,000 stories in total. I reviewed each and every submission, and while I had to narrow down my selections, I was honored to have the opportunity to glimpse into the musical lives of so many people.

The stories that follow were chosen not only because they are great works, but also because they complement one another very well. As I reviewed the submissions, I considered how the final pieces would be grouped together: should there be a chapter on healing, one on family traditions, another on travel? And so on. I quickly found that most works fall into more than one category, and organizing them in this way would limit the full impact of the individual stories.

So, I put that idea to rest. You will notice there are no chapters in this anthology; rather, I have arranged the stories to more subtly connect their themes to one another, which in a way, also mirrors our life cycle with music—how we come to experience it for the first time in youth, how we experience music as we age, and everything in between. And, like listening to an album, readers can follow the themes from beginning to end, or you can enjoy the individual works at random. The stories explore how music bonds us with our family and friends, the distinctive musical traditions in various cultures, how music can help us heal, and how it connects us to generations past and those yet to come, to people next door and others a world apart.

With works from more than forty authors and artists from eleven countries, *Stories of Music* will take you on a journey around the world through poetry, creative nonfiction, photography, audio recordings, and videos. These works will introduce you to fascinating people and perspectives; they will make you laugh, cry, and celebrate with the subjects of the stories; and they will arouse the music lover in you. Perhaps you will also be inspired to share *your* story. As part of the release of Volume 1, I have opened a new call for submissions for anyone who would like their work considered for publication in Volume 2. You can share your story at www.storiesofmusic.com.

Violin Improvisations

by Aleksandr Kuznetcov

This image represents improvisation, when the notes and scores are not important anymore—only thoughts, feelings, and memories . . . when the outer world disappears.

If These Walls Could Sing

by Steve Givens

If the walls of this old house could sing
you would hear ballads of birthdays
blues of passing lives
carols of great joy
pianos and fiddles like long ago riddles
echoing down its halls
bouncing along baseboards like mice trapped in the walls.

For what if
once played, once sung
music never really goes away
just hangs in the air
seeps into ceilings
becomes part of the furniture
like a drunken uncle who refuses to go home at the end of the night.

Just last week you sat there
by the fireplace
a guitar across your knee
a song flowing across your teeth and through your lips
filling the room with harmony
a dimly remembered past for someone else
in need of healing and restoration and rest.
Decades from now
a young mother will walk into this room
in desperate need of a lullaby
and hear the faint whisper of one
dripping from the brick and mortar of the hearth

and she will cock her head to one side
while she carries her son on her hip
and she will hum a song she has never heard before
and the boy will stop fidgeting and listen
to the now audible breath of his mother
and will glance at the fireplace as if there is something there
and smile
and wonder what it's all about
this life before him
filled with sound and echoes.

These walls can sing
do sing.
They put babies to sleep
bring in the New Year and lament the old.
They call out the tunes as the band begins to play
urging us to sing along
these songs we all know
somehow.
They cry out for one more
before we go
one for the road
just one more.

Music never dies.
It lives in the gaps of silence
if we're willing to be still
and listen.

When My Ears Began to Grow

by Ben Murray

time is the journey wind-sway cane makes
from the harvested field to factory to
the practiced lips and tongue of Cannonball Adderley
as he blows my seven-year-old mind, the sound
of his sax, my suburban Illinois savior

time is the four-bar break I take now, remembering

it's the late sixties, it's Chicago, Civil Rights are
marching on, and a post-King Jesse Jackson preaches
to the converts at Operation Breadbasket

but who, who is this white mother in bangs in
horn-rimmed Cat-Eye glasses with them?
she's *my* mother, she's my Holocaust-surviving mom
doing her bit to save this world and herself one raft
at a time

look real close and see us marching, hand in hand,
me some little blob of white in a sea of blackness, marching
down picketed streets, chanting "We Shall Overcome,"
the words foreign to me, the music a daylight lullaby
familiar as mom's gripping, guiding hand

around this time my earliest musical memory is born,
the music jazz is delivered to me, kissing and screaming
my four walls, Cannonball's *Accent On Africa*
taking first spins on our Woolworth's mono, and I swear
it's then when my ears really start to grow

it's a concept album, I know now, a jazz man's take
on African roots, a combo augmented by voices
by percussion by brass; but all I knew then was that
the exotic cover (a dashiki-clad Cannonball serenading some
neighborhood Nefertiti), and the magic black circle inside
held sustenance and shout-it-out power for my seven-year-old soul,
the misterioso tune, "Khutsana," still the music I want to hear
after I'm gone

like mama, like son I too did my world-changing bit:
with the help of Cannonball—cranking the lo-fi, front door open
wide to the world, I'd share the sounds, blasting the music
for passersby, album cover displayed porch-front as if to say,

Hey people, this is it, this is what you're hearing, listen
listen and change your life with me

The Music in Me

by Nolan Stevens

"The Music in Me" is a digital art piece which takes its cue from a 1974 photograph, and is inspired by the many effects music has on a person. It is able to add colour to our lives, almost always giving a zestful surge to anyone it touches. It can recall and create memories that last a lifetime, and it holds the power to unlock a variety of emotions which span from joyous elation to frantic aggression, and anything in between. In short, this piece is an ode to the many powers of music.

My Father's Sounds

by Robert William Iveniuk

Every time my father drove me through the Winnipeg streets, I understood where the songs came from. Each derelict building or forgotten alleyway had a story behind it, it seemed:

> See that rooftop? We peed on Big Moose when he was making out with his girlfriend up there. That house? My uncle bootlegged alcohol there. One of his customers shot a cop on the front porch. This bar was where I met a girl whose boyfriend was a demolitions guy for the army. My power went out four days later and I thought it was him, comin' for me!

My father, William Theodore Iveniuk, hails from what statisticians refer to as the Murder Capital of Canada, and one of my nation's most dangerous cities. Having grown up in the Eastern European-immigrant ghetto that was the notorious North End, my father lived a life that would be best described as a long-lost Samuel Beckett play re-enacted by the Kids in the Hall. Everything my father told me about his life made me wonder how he came out alive and relatively lucid.

Yet somehow, he did, and upon doing so made music. Influenced by Elvis Presley, Little Richard, and other founders of early rock 'n' roll, he put together a number of songs and toured with several bands, including Wild Rice and his personal project, Bill and The Bills. His music gained a cult following among a scant few, and had enough clout and creativity to write songs for Burton Cummings of the Guess Who and Sesame Street (the latter job was where he met my mother).

My father always played music for me, although according to him I was not privy to it at first. He recounted the ways I ran up to him to set a hand against the guitar strings, keeping him from strumming away. This seemed to pass quickly enough, as I mostly remember being serenaded with songs like "Mister Sandman" and artists like Harry Nilsson. To channel my frustrations, my father broke out his Gibson and helped me write music about things that bothered me.

To his disappointment, I'm not musically inclined. I have a passion for karaoke, to be sure, but my interest in picking up a guitar is limited due to a lack of confidence and skill, and my songwriting ability is laughable at best. And yet, living with a musician, hearing him grind out tunes in the studio he built in our basement, imparted a different kind of gift to me.

I was born with a learning disability. My cognitive and motor function skills are not as strong as they are in most people, and later in life I found myself at the mercy of a vicious anxiety disorder. Human interaction was, and at times still is, arduous for me, as I can find myself struggling to decipher people's words, thoughts, and feelings.

I became more curious about music as I aged, and soon acquired an eclectic taste. A controlling older brother only allowed me to listen to Europop until I was twelve, upon which time I stumbled across more aggressive artists like The Prodigy, Rob Zombie, and AC/DC, and the strange but familiar sounds of Japanese pop-rock. Music helped me channel my thoughts, encouraging me to be creative in other ways—taking up a pen to draw out a scene, or writing a story and setting it to music. Moreover, it helped me understand my peers, equating songs to certain situations or people, and when my more musically inclined classmates started producing their own music, their own sounds, I understood them even more.

When I hear my father's sounds, I understand him.

The music my father produced in his early days reflected the mad energy and rockabilly lifestyle he lived. The ultimate manifestation of this was found on the only full album Bill and The Bills produced, *Bills, Bills, Bills*, full of earworm-worthy tracks with lyrical content that ranged from love ballads to comedy. They carried whimsy, a carefree attitude, and a desire to love and be loved.

The songs my father wrote for himself later would change, and with reason. Since *Bills, Bills, Bills*, my father experienced hardship

> "There's a side to art that people are prone to neglect: the preservation of history. Not just world history and culture, but also personal history."

after hardship: raising two boys who had problems in school and life; forcing himself to work extra hard to help out around the house, injuring himself and wearing his body down more and more; and, the biggest blow, losing close friends, siblings, and even my half-sister. Though he doesn't say it, I know he feels the weight.

As such, when he got back to personal songwriting, there was a strong shift in tone, in soul. I'm not sure that these songs will ever see the light of day, but they are strong in my mind: "A Little Closer to Memphis," about a solemn Elvis Presley's return home from touring; "Meet Me at the Bridge," the story of a final farewell between two lifelong friends; and, "Beyond the Universe," a song that wonders about what lies, as he puts it, "beyond the golden gates." Even his more lighthearted songs, "Get a Hold of Yourself" and "If I Had a Clone," would not be out of place at some ho-down at the end of the world. They are somber and reflective and show the sadness in his heart.

There's a side to art that people are prone to neglect: the preservation of history. Not just world history and culture, but also personal history. How many songs came right from the heart, or were based on some aspect of the songwriter's life? What was the sociocultural zeitgeist that birthed that event, or the songwriter's way of thinking? Wouldn't you, the listener, want to know why a song was written, or who a song was written for? For me, it can enrich the experience. "Tears in Heaven," for example, became more tragic when I learned it was about the death of Eric Clapton's son, in much the same way I know (or think I know) who my father is talking to in "Meet Me at the Bridge."

Art, in this sense, creates both a window to the soul and a pocket in time. Songs in particular capture the voice of a musician, or the sound of their soul, and preserve it for future generations. Thanks to modern technology, we can actually capture a musician's voice so we can play it for the world to listen.

I'm thankful that my father recorded himself, preserved both his old and new songs. I'm thankful that I have his soul on tape. Hearing his music and singing his songs to myself breathes life into his memories of the sordid Winnipeg streets, shows me his scars, and tells me his secrets.

I'm thankful for my father's sounds, for they helped me to understand everyone else's.

The Accordionist
by Brut Carniollus

This digital collage is a portrait of
accordionist Jure Tori in action.

Street Music

by Anna Alferova

This photograph captures street musicians performing in the center of Moscow in the summer of 2013.

A Short Walk through Music's Long History:
Musicians on foot, past and present

by Benjamin Allmon

"Robert was a guy, you could wake him up at any time and he was ready to go . . . he wouldn't exchange no words with you. He's just ready to go . . . it didn't make him no difference. Just so he was going."
—Johnny Shines, Delta bluesman and travelling partner of Robert Johnson in the mid-1930s.

"Originally, we just wanted an alternative to touring in a van," said Raianne Richards, a folk musician from Massachusetts. In 2010, she and Mark Mandeville embarked upon an eighteen-day, 180-mile trek across their home state, playing tiny towns and sleeping rough. Thus began the Massachusetts Walking Tour, now an annual event. "We had a few friends who had done 'human-powered' tours by bicycle or canoe, so this inspired us to try a walking tour."

In so doing, they were re-enacting a musical tradition that goes back a long, long way. There were the Delta bluesmen of the early twentieth century, ramblers such as Robert Johnson, Tommy Johnson, and Charlie Patton who took to the roads and rails during the Great Migration. There were the balladeers of Victorian England, stunningly captured in Mayhew's *London Labour and the London Poor*, in which he interviewed dozens of street musicians, the most arresting of whom was Old Sarah. A

blind hurdy-gurdy woman who had played the streets of London for over forty years, she was an irrepressible soul who, despite her meagre earnings, supported two or three pensioners poorer than herself.

Sarah and her fellows were the descendants of the minstrels of Europe's medieval roads, entertainers who plied their trade for hundreds of years until the sixteenth century saw their role subsumed and divided by specialisation and other art forms, principally theatre. There were the troubadours and *trobairitz* of the Middle Ages, and the *gleemen* and *scop* of the Dark Ages who roamed the land before them. Buskers, street poets, and *histriones* trod the highways of the Roman Empire, Republic and Kingdom long before that.

Before any language we now understand, before the domestication of animals, before the Agricultural Revolution, musicians have been travelling the countryside. At about 40,000 years old, the bird bone flutes of Geißenklösterle in southern Germany are the earliest archaeological evidence we have of instrumentation. Of course, such instrument crafting must have been going on long before that, as well as singing, which leaves no trace . . . other than the neurological evidence. The capacity for creating and interpreting music—the changes in the brain, aural, and vocal systems—occurred at least 300,000 years ago, before our species, *Homo sapiens*, existed.

***

Occurring each summer, the Massachusetts Walking Tour is always accompanied by a unique artwork by another New England musician, Dan Blakeslee.

This marriage of art and music is similarly ancient. In fact, 22,000 years ago, during the peak of the last Ice Age, humans decorated the walls of the Niaux cave, amongst many others in the Pyrenees, with paintings of the animals they hunted or were following along migratory routes. These prehistoric Dan Blakeslees, however, weren't the only creative, nomadic hunter-gatherers in these shadowy, fire-lit caves.

A study published by Iégor Reznikoff and Michel Dauvois in 1988 revealed that the paintings were usually within one metre of the point of the best resonance in the cave—a phenomenon that would have enhanced any instrument, but particularly the range of the singing human voice. They kept searching; wherever there was art, there was a nearby point where the acoustics of the cave were optimal.

Furthermore, most points of resonance were accompanied by art, even in difficult-to-reach parts of the cave. Interestingly, walls deemed perfect for painting—but which were in aurally unsuitable locations—were left bare. The

> "It seems that the art and music were being conducted simultaneously."

researchers came to believe that the art and music had been performed simultaneously, because bone flutes like those in Geißenklösterle were found in these same caves, dated to the same time.

Not only that, there is evidence that the cave itself was an instrument. Reznikoff, Dauvois, and others have analysed stalactites and formations that bear marks from being struck; where each mark had been made, it produced a distinct tone that differed from its neighbours. These lithophones—"stone voices"—were often decorated with art themselves, as in Spain's Nerja caves, where a huge, concertina-like structure seems to have acted like an enormous stone organ, covered with art.

So what was going on in these caves? It seems that the art and music were being conducted simultaneously, and that this was initially a seasonal event—the evidence and deposits were heaviest around spring and autumn, indicating that it was possibly a gathering along migratory routes. Some, like Professor J. David Lewis-Williams, believe that the paintings were the product of shamans in

Massachusetts Walking Tour artwork by Dan Blakeslee

a music-induced trance, based on his study of contemporary hunter-gatherer societies. It may have been a communal activity, or a solitary one.

Whatever the case may be, the idea that ancient humans—just like present-day musicians, Richards, Mandeville, and Blakeslee—were congregating in caves at the glacial frontier to engage in Palaeolithic festivals of the arts is an intoxicating one. Life for these wandering musicians was not easy, however . . . nor would it be for their descendants.

***

When Richards and Mandeville embarked on their first hike on the first day of the Massachusetts Walking Tour, they traversed one of the steepest roads in the state for eighteen miles. "Our group of five became separated and one collapsed from exhaustion," Richards said. "We didn't have any sort of mobile support, so he did have to eventually finish his walk that day. We got to our first show two hours late, but the restaurateur still allowed us to 'sing for our supper.'" That night they camped behind the restaurant in a gravel lot near the river. Richards explained, "There was a bridge overhead that was actually a train trestle on which the train went by every two hours, all night long."

Despite this forbidding start to their journey they pushed on, forced to make the rapid adjustment the walking life imposes. But whereas most musicians—past and present—focus on furthering their own career or accumulating wealth, Richards and Mandeville discovered a far nobler reason to walk and play. Richards said, "Some of these towns hadn't had a concert of any kind for many years, in one case over twenty-five years. There was obviously a need not only to bring music to these communities, but also to create an opportunity for the local performers, poets, musicians, and artists, as well as those who coordinate these activities, to get together and showcase their local resources."

***

This idea of a great convergence of musicians is an old one, too. Back when Rome was just another small village dotting the Italian countryside, people would gather at harvest time at a place in the village known as the *compita*, or crossroads. Crossroads were important because they served as a natural meeting place, not just of people, but also of ideas. Such was their significance, shrines were erected to the *Lares Compitales*, or Gods of the Crossroads.

A festival grew up around these places of worship called the *Compitalia*, and this drew musicians from all over the countryside. A style of song emerged, known as the *fescennina*: a good-natured rap battle of sorts and a way of teasing someone in verse, often employed at weddings and harvests.

The significance of the crossroads continued as Rome grew into the centre of the ancient world; in areas of dense housing, the crossroads remained a place where people gathered, shrines were erected, and entertainers congregated. By then, however, the *fescennina*

> "Music in all its forms is too deeply embedded in human physiology and neurology, and the songs continued."

had become a tool of political machinery, a weapon that was effective precisely because of music's power over the emotions of the populace. It got so bad that in 451 BCE the Senate imposed the Twelve Tables, laws governing the people's behaviour, of which one was *libelli famosi*—the banning of these songs and writings of abuse—which carried with it the penalty of death.

Of course, it did not succeed. Music in all its forms is too deeply embedded in human physiology and neurology, and the songs continued. In 27 BCE, Augustus Caesar restored the *Compitalia*, which at that point was no longer a small rural event but a festival much like today's Lollapalooza or SXSW, if we consider Dio Chrysostom's account of street life in the first century:

> *And I remember once seeing, while walking through the Hippodrome, many people on one spot and each one doing something different: one playing the flute, another dancing, another doing a juggler's trick, another reading a poem aloud, another singing, and another telling some story or myth . . .*

This is from his Twentieth Discourse and illustrates how the *Compitalia* had grown with Rome and yet remained essentially unchanged over the centuries; it was a vibrant place where all forms of artistic expression were conducted and where wandering musicians found a home.

***

The *Compitalia* was not able to survive without the funding of the state, and today little has changed. The Massachusetts Walking Tour (in its sixth year at the time of this writing) is only possible through a combination of cultural grants, funds from the Friends of the Library and other community groups, donations, and a lot of hard work by Richards and Mandeville. In keeping with their altruistic approach, the shows are free. "All in all, it mostly pays for itself," Richards said.

This economic neutrality is helped by the kindness of strangers. "People are very supportive of us and go out of their way to be kind. We have had people leave us watermelon or even a cooler full of cold drinks and snacks . . . trail magic, I believe it's called."

***

There was trail magic during the *Compitalia* in the form of honeycakes left at the crossroads, although they were for the Gods, not the musicians, according to Dionysius of Halicarnassus. But the encouragement for wandering musicians to ply their trade by those who are stationary is an impulse for which we see evidence time and again, even when the law forbids it.

Indeed, it is the everyday townsfolk who have kept the music—and thus the wandering musicians—alive through some of the most brutally oppressive regimes humanity has concocted. The Romans' *libelli famosi* had a negligible effect despite it carrying the death penalty. The alliance of Church and State a thousand years later under Charlemagne and the Holy Roman Empire resulted in a decree, enforced most enthusiastically by his son, Louis I, which effectively outlawed the music of the people. This, too, had little effect (not helped by the fact that those in power usually kept musicians themselves whilst forbidding music for everyone else).

Religious persecution of musicians—from the Eastern Orthodox Church's campaign against Russia's *skomorokh*, to the Roman Catholic Church's crusade against the troubadours of southern France—dented not one whit the people's desire for their music. It was only when the people no longer desired their music that the *skomorokh* declined, whilst the troubadours' demise was hastened by the church-sanctioned Albigensian Crusade in 1229 and sealed by the Black Death a century later.

In the centuries that followed, royalty, governments, and churches across Europe imposed ordinances, decrees, and laws to forbid the practice of the street musician, and whilst partially successful on a case-by-case basis, could best be deemed a stalemate. Even the establishment of Minstrel Guilds, whom travelling entertainers had to join or else abstain from playing, struggled to achieve their aim.

But perhaps no attempt to forbid people from making the music they loved was as brutal and as unsuccessful as the slave codes of eighteenth-century America, whereby the African slaves were forbidden from performing their music—particularly drum-based methods

"People's desire for music, through all ages, is like water through rock—it always finds a way through, regardless of what is in its way."

of communication, which hearkened back to the country from which they had been taken—as it was seen to be a spark for rebellion, a musical language not understood by the slave owners. Bereft of their drums, these earliest African-Americans transferred these rhythms to everyday household items such as spoons and washboards, and they even slapped their own bodies in a dance known as "Juba."

Their need to sing emerged as spirituals, which weren't banned as they were seen as evidence of the Christianisation of the black people; but this music, too, contained rebellious elements—everything from messages of unity and support for one another to messages of revolt and directions to the Underground Railroad. From this blend of spiritual singing, lyrical metaphor, concealed messages, and rhythmic propulsion came the ingredients for the genres that followed: jazz, blues, gospel, and R&B.

People's desire for music, through all ages, is like water through rock—it always finds a way through, regardless of what is in its way, and this desire has ensured the wandering musician's continued existence.

***

The relentless nature of water is something Richards has grown used to: "Rain can be difficult, but thunderstorms are worse. June always has some . . . one year we were rained on for almost the whole tour, and it's a challenge keeping the instruments dry. The last few years we have had to secure venues that have an 'in case of rain' option."

That said, they do not exclusively play booked gigs. "When walking through towns, it's always pleasurable to stop and talk with passersby,

"Wandering was, and is, an excellent way of driving the evolution of music through exposure to different styles."

or maybe even sing an *a cappella* tune. We perform acoustically, so we have challenges with our performance locations being close to a busy road."

By posting their itinerary online and inviting others—musicians or hikers—to join in also has the advantage of keeping things fresh for Richards and Mandeville, as well as staving off the loneliness (and danger) of travelling alone.

"Since we have different musicians accompany us each year our repertoire changes each year as well," Richards added.

***

Perhaps the greatest benefit of being a wandering musician is that by travelling to foreign lands, often in the company of musicians with different skill sets, one's own music incorporates these new influences. This was the essence of the crossroads of ancient Rome, and it was summed up perfectly in the writings of Widsith (which means "far traveller") sometime in the seventh century when he wrote, "The makar's wierd is to be a wanderer: the poets of mankind go through many countries. . . ."

Makar refers to "one who makes," which is the meaning of the word *scop*, the bards of the Teutonic people, whilst "wierd" is their word for fate. The *scop* were responsible for the number-one hit of the Dark Ages, *Beowulf*. The *gleemen* (the Teutonic version of the Roman street performer), or *histriones* (actors), spread these songs of heroism and glorious battles as they traipsed across Europe.

The Widsith poem is part of the *Exeter Book*, the largest surviving collection of Old English literature, and was donated to the Exeter Cathedral in 1072. This was six years after another wandering musician, Taillefer, played a prominent role in the event that changed Britain forever: the Battle of Hastings.

Taillefer was a minstrel, a class of entertainer who emerged from the tradition of the *gleemen* and *scop*, and the minstrels had their own number-one hit, "The Song of Roland." As William the Conqueror's minstrel, Taillefer apparently sang it as he led the charge that saw the Normans overthrow the Anglo-Saxons and forever change the shape of England's culture. He was also the first Norman casualty.

Taillefer was not the only musician who got himself mixed up in war. One hundred forty years later, William IX, Duke of Aquitaine and a troubadour, led an army in the disastrous Crusade of 1101. So poor was his military acumen that on one occasion his entire force was annihilated—only he and a few others narrowly escaped the Battle of Heraclea.

But William IX isn't remembered for his military prowess or lack thereof; he was the first troubadour whose work survived, and he formulated a new genre of music precisely because of his travels through the Muslim world. Exposed to their music during the Crusade, and with his Duchy of Aquitaine neighbouring the Moorish kingdom of Islamic Spain, William IX took a great deal of influence from the Muslim *raouis*, or storytellers, of the twelfth century.

Whilst Europe was still labouring under the hangover of *Beowulf* and *chansons de geste* like "The Song of Roland," the Muslims were using music to express their appreciation for the beauty of the world—the natural world, the seasons, and women.

William IX's main claim to fame was his fusion of the northern European song structure—better suited for storytelling—with the subject matter of the romantic Muslims to the south. In so doing, he and his contemporaries spawned a genre of music that was to become known as the "songs of love," which for the next two centuries accompanied a movement known as chivalry. Women and love have remained at the heart of lyrical composition ever since.

Wandering was, and is, an excellent way of driving the evolution of music through exposure to different styles. And whilst it is true that the musician's fate is to be a wanderer, it is not because of some urge to stroll about the countryside looking windswept and interesting, but because it is the only way to reach new revenue sources. Simply put, very few towns have an economy large enough to support a full-time busker. The life of a wandering musician is only sustainable if the musician keeps wandering, and far from romantic, it is about survival.

***

Richards sees the concept of sustainability this way:

I actually think it would be easier to make a living in terms of costs versus profit, touring in this way, but it is much harder to do. There are many, many trails across America and lots of possibilities. When we are on the road it's hard enough to keep up with booking . . . [needing] regular access to the Internet . . . I can't imagine what it would be like to organise something like this [while] traveling on foot.

So why do it? Richards feels there is something this method of touring gives not just performers, but the audience (and townsfolk), that regular touring doesn't:

The walking aspect of this, though exhausting, does change my attitude. First of all, getting to perform that show at the end of the day is very satisfying and makes all those blisters and sunburn hardly noticeable. After spending most of the day in the woods, even small things like getting to use an actual restroom or having a real sit-down meal seem like luxury! I take a lot less for granted when doing this so when it comes time to perform I feel like we really pour ourselves into it and squeeze every last bit out.

And what about when it's over? "The last show is always bittersweet," Richards said. "While we are usually exhausted after it's over, I always feel like, 'So now I have to go back to regular life in the regular world?'"

***

Some never did. For some, wandering *became* their life, forever on the move. Nowhere is this evidenced more than in the Delta bluesmen of the Great Migration. Men like Charlie Patton and Robert Johnson are the most well known of this breed of rambler that emerged in the wake of Reconstruction in the South, in the first decades of the twentieth century. Patton, who was born late in the nineteenth century (nobody knows the exact date for sure), was the physical distillation of the American story: part white, part black, and part Cherokee. In the musical sense, he was also the distillation of the many styles and influences that surrounded him, able to turn his hand to ragtime, jump-ups, folk, spirituals, and of course, blues. Patton only gained a proficiency in these various genres because he travelled widely within the Delta and fulfilled that other crucial role of the wandering musician: giving the people what they want.

Johnson may have played with Patton toward the end of Patton's career, but whether he learned from him or not, he certainly adopted the life, and to an even greater degree. Roaming as far as Canada, Johnson truly was the epitome of the rambling musician, and not just because he was always on the move. Johnson could play anything the audience wanted, from Polish folk songs to polkas, as his travelling companion and fellow bluesman, Johnny Shines shared: "Well, you had to do it . . . lots of times you wake up in the morning and you didn't have no money at all. Somebody ask you to play a song, maybe they'd give you a dollar . . . that meant about four meals . . . and if you couldn't play that song, you miss that money. So you had to learn to play some of everything you heard."

There were many other ramblers in those days, men who lived a largely rootless existence, and for the most part they were hard men, made so by the rigors of life on the road. It is not an easy life, but for many of them it was infinitely preferable to sharecropping or labouring in the turpentine camps or levee building. Once those options had been abandoned, there was little else to do.

And perhaps *that* is the greatest danger of the walking musician's life—not the walking, not the long road and all its hidden dangers, but the inability to do anything else after awhile, of reintegrating with society. Going back to the regular world, as Richards calls it.

Those musicians of the Great Migration gave the people who heard them a brief reprieve from the harshness of their own lives, which in some ways was every bit as hard as it had been under slavery. The ability to transport people away from their immediate troubles is perhaps the noblest aspect to the life of the musician, wandering or not. Or, maybe it is simply as Richards noted: "I think that many get wrapped up in the romanticism of our gypsy-like tour . . . we really are travelling minstrels. People hear our music and our story and you can see that sparkle in their eyes. They can live a little of it through our experience."

Scan to Watch

or visit
www.sombk.co/v1/27

"Lost in Walden" on the Massachusetts Walking Tour

This video captures Raianne Richards and Mark Mandeville during the 5th Annual Massachusetts Walking Tour (2014) as they make a stop at the Thoreau Institute at Walden Woods in Lincoln, Massachusetts. In this video, Richards and Mandeville perform "Follow the Drinking Gourd" and "Hard Times and Woes" with Mark Kilianski and Amy Alvey.

Video by James Kelly and Richard Kelly, used with permission from Raianne Richards

Learn more about the Massachusetts Walking Tour and the artists behind the organization:
www.masswalkingtour.org, www.markmandeville.com, www.danblakeslee.com

Massachusetts Walking Tour, 2015
(photo courtesy of Raianne Richards)

In the Tunnel at the End of the Day

by Stephanie Reitano

The dark hole that pours out people
Like a gravity-defying waterfall
Had a heartbeat that day
Barely audible on the surface
Fighting rush-hour traffic to get in
Where the world was getting out
Lured deeper underground
By the echo of a soul
Walking past the platform
Drawn to the rhythm
Like only those whose minds hear in color can be
It grew louder, defiant
Begging to be heard over the stomping herd of human cattle
Yet, whispering its song through the veins of all who cared to listen
Against the wall
Out of the way, almost unseen
There on a milk crate
With a bucket and a stick
Sat a boy with worn out sneakers
The deep sound of air caught in a drum
The high pitch of a stick on the edge
The melodius rise and fall
Of fingers and palms on the smooth surface
Garbage, an old, used five-gallon bucket
A twig and broken milk crate
Still, in this tunnel sat a boy
Whose heartbeat echoed in the corridor
The only time I ever gladly missed a train

Watching the trains pass by (photo by Eutah Mizushima)

Migrating between Song Lines

by Debra Raver

The Great Divide

A great white bison once roamed this Wyoming river basin, enticing natives to name it "Gray Bull." Wildlife still migrate up and down the area, wintering down in the Greybull River watershed along the Bighorn Range. My father and his father were born here, as was I, the first of five daughters.

My mother's folks were farming people; they tended crops near the shores of Neringa, named after a Lithuanian sea goddess. The feminine soul runs deep in Lithuania. *Sutartinès*, polyphonic chants created by women, once flourished there. Village women would weave their musical threads tightly together, crossing notes over and under in parallel seconds to create a distinct clash between two voices. Only through the closest point of relationship could they reach agreement.

For much of my life I knew nothing about Lithuania at all, because Stalin's iron fence of communism had cordoned off the borders. But I sensed a cultural dissonance snaking through my body, an unwieldy root with a strange scent like sea sage, born of neither home.

Now I travel back and forth between Wyoming and Lithuania, piecing together my heritage as women used to weave the songlines of *sutartinès*. This is the story of my own migration route, of the women who stood on separate sides, and of the music that helped mediate my passage through the divide.

The Displaced Persons Act of 1948 paved the way for the passage of roughly 200,000 displaced persons to the United States. My grandmother Marie arrived by ship to Ellis Island with her children Marianne and Martin in tow; from there they made their way westward to their new home near Basin, Wyoming.

Reconciliation did not come easy for a woman who had endured Hitler's promises in Memel's market square in 1939, and who had survived the German DP camps. It made her a pretty tough bird. Marie never did accept her life in America. When I visited her in Lithuania, after she returned at age eighty-seven to reclaim her family's farmstead, she announced resolutely, her eyes blazing, "I would rather live in Moscow than move back to America!"

They met at a roller skating rink in Greybull. Edward, a dark-haired American boy, asked Marianne to drag Main in his `52 Oldsmobile. Things really heated up after that. One day Marie flew into a rage and smashed an Elvis record (a loving gift to Marianne from Ed) into pieces. The two lovers left a note on the kitchen table and eloped to Billings. From that day forward my mother officially crossed over to my father's world; my grandmother remained in another.

I remember how Mother stuttered slightly when she was nervous, a remnant of an earlier trauma: the terrors she saw running with Marie past bombed-out buildings and bodies, barely escaping bombs themselves as they sought shelter each night. Marianne considered Wyoming her "real" home. Her wish was that her ashes "absolutely not" be scattered in some ungodly spot in Lithuania, so far from Wyoming—the place she had adopted as her safe haven.

One could say that, until the end of the Cold War, it was the Soviets that barred me from entering Lithuania. But it was the static electricity whenever the homeland was brought up—that morphic field of dread that would emanate from my mother and wipe out her smile—that became the barbed iron fence in my home and first taught me of borders that could not safely be crossed.

First Migration

In May of 1997, out of the blue, Marie suddenly brought up the subject of Lithuania. "Why don't we go there together?" she asked me.

I have a photograph of Grandmother holding both hands against her head in disbelief the moment she realized we had found her family farm. We returned to the States with little jars of soil as souvenirs. But within three months, Marie was again on a plane to Lithuania, with all her belongings in her suitcases, back to the only home she'd ever claimed. My mother never saw her again.

That trip in 1997 unleashed the floodgates for me as well. I had only to open the door, and all the world of Lithuania rose up to meet me.

Second Migration

September 1999. I've returned to Lithuania to try songwriting with Žemyna, a woman who plays the *kanklės*, a Lithuanian zither-like instrument. I compose the text during a series of late nights in my grandmother's attic. "They came from distant shores, singing peace . . . Dobilio," I would sing softly into my tape recorder, while Grandma snored downstairs.

December. Sigitas is coming to Grandmother's house for dinner. We've been dating for several weeks now. I stare out the window towards the dots of tiny village homes that had been built up over Marie's property

> "'They came from distant shores, singing peace . . . Dobilio,' I would sing softly into my tape recorder, while Grandma snored downstairs."

during Soviet times, hoping all goes well. But soon my grandmother launches her attacks. "Are you Lutheran?" she fired at Sigitas.

"I am Catholic," he answered.

"So, how can you claim you are from Klaipėda area, Prussian territory?"

A look passed over his eyes; he knew where this was going. Not backing down, he replied proudly, "I live here now, but I was born in Žemaitija." There. He had said the words aloud. "Žemaitis. A lowlander." Only the Lutherans could be of Old Prussian stock like my grandmother.

Then she started in on me, the "tramp." When all was said and done, I'd stormed out of the house. It was cold, with lots of snow, and there was no bus in sight, as I hadn't timed things properly. When Sigitas caught up to me, he implored me to return to the house. "She is your Grandmother! You must go back." But I took one heel and dug it across the snow hard and fast.

"Don't you see this line?" I was thinking, "I cannot go back there; I refuse to allow her poisonous words into my body, to fester like the cancer growing inside my mother."

Facing Grandmother had always been fearsome because of the wall of piety she projected. I return to Wyoming feeling war torn. My mother understands. We share many

"Sometimes I feel like a strange bird—a jumbled mass of feathers with legs longer than my body from wading between worlds."

conversations that February, drinking sweet tea, curled up in easy chairs overlooking the Bighorn Mountains. She confides in me that she once saw my chaste grandmother kissing the man who had sponsored their immigration to Wyoming.

So, Grandmother was human after all! I thank my mother for sharing this family secret, and say, "Your stories change everything."

"They do . . . ?" She paused and added in genuine wonderment, "I never really thought they would make any difference."

March 18, 2000. Wyoming: Mother dies of cancer.
December 14, 2000. Lithuania: Grandmother dies of heart failure.
December 15, 2000. Wyoming: I become the new matriarch.

Third Migration

November 2001. Sigitas and I travel to my grandmother's gravesite near Klaipėda to light candles on Velinės, a time to honor the dead. I pray for forgiveness from the woman whom I could not forgive. Twilight falls. Here in this ancient graveyard of my ancestors, sky and earth mingle as one inside a flickering dance of shadow and light. The image of that cold hard line breaking open the snow that day pulses in my memory as I once again make my way to Grandmother's bus stop, with not a soul to stop me.

In Vilnius, I receive an unprecedented invitation to study with a group of women learning *sutartinės* at The Lithuanian Academy of Music and Theatre. I arrive to find I am the only person in the room who speaks English. Until my Lithuanian improves, I must learn to communicate solely through *sutartinės*.

The semester comes and goes, and the class takes a vacation. My language skills are getting a little better. I buy better sound

34

equipment. Come February 2002, when the class reconvenes, I am ready to capture these songs on digital media and record my observations in more detail.

I discover that twentieth-century villagers described *sutartinės* as "terribly beautiful," like birdsong. Recordings of their canonic refrains echo the polyphonic language of the water birds they imitated, remnants of ancient rites symbolizing the bridge between human and divine.

I recall how Mother loved the honking of her geese, and how Grandmother, too, was fond of "beerdts" (as she pronounced it). "Storks never roost at a bad person's house," she would say. As I burrow more deeply into my research, I uncover a peculiar sort of *sutartinė*, a totemic ode to the Mother Duck, Untytė. It is structured by parts that are piped to represent a family of birds. In this *sutartinė*, the voices of the ancestors reverberate alongside the rest of the family. The individual pipes depend upon Untytė, the matriarch, but when pieced together they sound as a melodious whole. Without this cooperation between parts, the song collapses.

I begin meeting with the folklore ensemble Verdingis to practice "The Harvest Song," a raw weave between the poem "Rugpjūtis," a *sutartinė*, and my own music. We rehearse in a schoolhouse near the TV tower where in 1991, Soviet troops challenged Lithuania's independence by gunning down thirteen civilians.

In June 2003, Verdingis invites me to debut "The Harvest Song" at an outdoor concert. I look out upon a sea of Lithuanian people as we begin singing our song of solidarity: "Hope and fortitude will bud, when this season is renewed, the scythe will shine not with blood, but with the harvest's silvery dew." My birthday arrives the next day, and Joninės, the Solstice. I wake feeling as if my time here has come to fruition.

Autumn 2003: I must leave half my baggage behind with Sigitas, but I make sure to get my recordings home in one piece, just in time for Thanksgiving.

A Place between Places

Sometimes I feel like a strange bird—a jumbled mass of feathers with legs longer than my body from wading between worlds. I seem gangly and awkward, as if the rest of me has yet to catch up with these mutant sea legs. I feel like a creature floating between hemispheres, as I strive in my day-to-day routine to interact with my Wyoming community through this incoherent "beaksong." Perhaps I need to just breathe for a spell. A white picket fence borders my long-time Laramie apartment. For now, I can rest here.

Riversong Studio, 2005. My four sisters and I gather to record "*Ėjau*: Through Fields to My Mother" in a studio near Sheridan, Mother's final resting place. We stand in a circle. Below us, twin creeks run parallel through the forest. The song weaves back and forth between the traditional *sutartinė* and my original lyrics: "Ėjau Rytelia Čiuta . . . I walk in the morning, through fields to my mother, take away her burden . . . Čiuta!" I am not surprised to find that our voices have a way of meshing when we reach a certain point of concentration. In olden times only women of the same tribe sang *sutartinės*. We each wear a beaded bracelet to symbolize our connection to each other, and to those who sang in circles before us.

I have now crossed the ocean six times. I no longer have a grandmother to meet me as I fly east, no welcoming mother to greet my return to the west. Only lingering echoes between their voices remain, weaving my life's polyphonic refrain in a way that grows "terribly beautiful" with each crossing. As I migrate between songlines, through their disparity, I am slowly learning the art of mediation.

Soon I will receive dual citizenship papers, and this betrothal between fatherland and motherland will be official. I'm still searching for a way to continue my research on *sutartinės*; I still plan to finish "Žemė," a prayer to the Earth, from the organ music I recorded inside Lithuania's oldest Lutheran church.

Like *sutartinės*, the songlines I'm lacing have no definitive end, woven as they are from the timeless fragments of birdsong. But I have learned to believe in the wisdom of old village women, and the sheer magic of intention. I can only trust that the Earth will continue to cycle me through each new threshold, and that I will be given courage to face the next uncertain hour. I carry the knowledge that I've tested the gates between two worlds and have learned that they *do* swing in both directions; I am becoming my own fence line.

I once wove summer grasses into a wreath and set it free down the Neris River on a day when the sun strayed so long from the sky that it met the moonrise. Some say the fate of a wreath as it makes its way down a riverbank, a place between places, can portend a marriage. It is precisely at these sojourns between boundaries that one can still join the solstice of women who turn towards the setting sun to honor the world behind, towards the rising moon to face the world beyond, and toss their wreaths with hopeful abandon into the dark but moving waters.

Scan to Listen

or visit
www.sombk.co/v1/37a

"The Harvest Song"
by Debra Raver

Scan to Listen

or visit
www.sombk.co/v1/37b

"Ėjau"
by Debra Raver

Recorded in Vilnius, Lithuania, and co-produced with Giedrius Klimka, "The Harvest Song" combines traditional Lithuanian folk melodies, motifs, and poetic influences (Justinas Marcinkevičius) with song material composed and performed by Debra Raver (guitar and lead vocals). The cooperative spirit of harvest time is expressed by the lively voices and instruments of the native folk musicians that perform with Raver (the Verdingis ensemble and cellist Gediminas Alekna). The song evokes Lithuania's history of war and the Soviet occupation but envisions a renewed harvest and hope for group harmony.

"Ėjau" is a multi-layered weave between a Lithuanian folk song (*sutartinė*) and original lyrics and music composed by Debra Raver. Since in older times only women of the same clan chanted *sutartinės*, Raver and her four sisters (Syna, Laurie, Eydie, and Marjorie) who harmonize on this recording echo their Lithuanian mother's deep musical heritage. This motif is carried through the song's narrative: "Ėjau . . . I walked in the morning, through fields to my mother, to take away her burden, Čiuta."

For Fourteen Hands

by Jari Thymian

At the Musical Instrument Museum—
a video shows six women standing up to their waists

in water that surrounds one of Vanuatu's islands.

They play the sea as a percussion instrument, slapping
the waves at different angles and speeds in a water

symphony for twelve hands in prisms of light and sound.

Hands that earlier cleaned fish, scrubbed clothes in tubs,
started fires to cook rice, now play the South Pacific.

Why had I not seen, a drum doesn't need a skin,

just water's surface tension? Songs of bathwater,
summer legato on a small lake, cadences I've poured

away, deftly dismissed with deafness. Now I bow

to cup my hands, wash my face in rhythms without
a vanishing point. Now I bow to join hands with these women,

musicians praising water at depths I've not fathomed before.

The Music Trade

by Patricia J. Esposito

(On seeing the band Train Company play at North Side Summer Fest)

If the old Silk Road of crimson, blue,
and gold, the carted sunrise of religions

melding, wagons carrying calligraphy
and constellations, if all was lost to disease

and the calculated course of commodities,
can it be found again in this nomadic singer

traversing blues, jazzy roads, and rock—
the roll of what lures his silken voice to weave?

He, with the rhythmic loom he strums, twines
heart with heart, no strained cocoon in his free-

flow shine, no streamlined greed as he plucks
new passages. He sings an open road, spins

for us a new cloak, teaches to reflect the light
unknotted, a new trade route thriving: a note

for a listening ear, a smile for a smile, as he
bends to thread his heart to string and pipes

a lustrous invitation to bridge, to stitch, to sing.

Train Company (photo courtesy of Rob Lejman)

My Heart Still Thinks of Yesterday

by Lapis

Scan to Listen
or visit
www.sombk.co/v1/42

"My Heart Still
Thinks of Yesterday"
by Lapis

"My Heart Still Thinks of Yesterday" invokes a philosophy of classical Hindustani music based on separation—the separation we feel when we are born and are no longer one with the source of our creation, and the separation we feel when our loved ones leave us here on Earth to return to this source.

Lapis members from left to right: Rup Sidhu, Mohamed Assani, and Curtis Andrews (photo courtesy of Rup Sidhu)

Indian Classical Music

by Bhaskar Das

Indian Classical music—an art form comprising vocal, dance, and instrumental performances—is one of the richest music forms in the world where you find a nuptial knot between art and mathematics, body and mind, human beings and the Almighty.

Music in His Blood

by Ata Mohammad Adnan

Ratan, pictured in white, has been singing since his childhood, a gift from his ancestors. Now, he travels from one village to another in Bangladesh to sing, and make a living in the process.

Street Musician
by Chinmoy Biswas

This photograph was taken in Varanasi where this snake charmer was performing to earn a living.

A Dialog of Echoes

by Darrin DuFord

Diesel smoke, grill smoke, cigarette smoke. They were just warm-ups for a face full of fumes from burning cardboard and furniture. At the curb, I stood over the flames, too enchanted to seek fresher air. A burly Iranian man urged me to draw from a soda bottle refilled with red wine as a girl I had never met greeted me with a kiss on the cheek.

It was Friday night in Montevideo, Uruguay, and I was waiting for the candombe drum group Tambor Brujo to begin its weekly march through otherwise quiet streets. Over a dozen drummers had placed their drums sideways around the fire so the heat would tune up the horsehide heads. "It's like Jimi Hendrix," a scruffily-bearded drummer commented to me when he threw a newspaper into the fire. Unlike Hendrix's guitar, the drums themselves remained singe-free, their heads glowing in the firelight like setting suns.

Barrel-shaped and ribbed with metal rings, the candombe drum looks and sounds similar to the conga, since both claim a common origin in the traditions of Bantu peoples of Africa, brought to Uruguay and Cuba as slaves. The group waiting around the fire, however, reflected the ethnic makeup of modern Uruguay: mostly white. Just as blues in America is no longer race specific, so went candombe in Uruguay.

Nor is candombe gender specific. Nor fashion specific. Aside from a few drummers wearing red Tambor Brujo t-shirts, the sartorial hodge-podge espoused Montevideo's standard casual style: cargo shorts, jeans, loafers, flip flops. Painted drum designs ranged from flames to hammers and sickles. The group stood like a ragtag band about to support a ragtag army, without the army.

Tambor Brujo is one of many candombe groups that marches through the city's streets each week. During Carnival, each group, or *cuerda*, dons matching costumes and day-glow face paint. But tonight, in mid-March, the idea was just to go out and drum.

I approached Lalo, a drummer who also administers websites for Uruguayan musicians. While he was collecting his instrument from the fire, I asked him if the drums bother the neighbors. Without looking up, he answered, "They're accustomed."

Accustomed. An ominously ambiguous word choice. It could mean that the people have given up, have found some lip-biting way of coping. Many Americans, for example, have become accustomed to their families and friends hunching over smartphones at the dinner table.

When the group began to march and the cracks of sticks striking tight skin began bouncing between façades, I learned what accustomed meant. Flip-flop-wearing residents walked out onto the sidewalk to watch. Toddlers with tyke-sized candombe drums strapped onto them waited in thresholds, egged on by their parents to play along.

Meanwhile, several young women had begun squirming in a hip-whipping dance in front of the drummers, albeit wearing considerably more fabric than during Carnival. People walking their dogs steered their pets alongside the *cuerda*. Couples circled while snapping photos, the *cuerda* gaining mass with each block.

I followed the sounds of the drums ricocheting off the houses. The walls seemed alive, responding to the drums in perfect time. As a percussionist, I caught a naughty thrill hearing the irresistibly sweet—and often forbidden—marriage of drums and street acoustics. That was when I noticed Pocitos—this residential neighborhood—was noticeably well kept, showing off its bright window trim and proud, lush trees. I thought of David Byrne's ruminations in his *Bicycle Diaries* concerning the usual correlation between a neighborhood's affordability and its tolerance for eccentricity. I wished he could have joined us, bike and all. As a side benefit of choosing a pleasant urban neighborhood for drumming, there's a steady supply of slightly used, discarded furniture to burn when it comes time to tune up.

Drums being tuned by the fire

The *cuerda* successfully blocked traffic, forcing cars to crawl at the pace of the synchronized steps. No one honked. No obscene gestures stabbed the air. Some cars refused to remain silent, however, owing to the degree of affluence that ushers in inevitable car alarms. The rumble of bass from the larger drums set the alarms of parked cars a-squealing, that awful robotic blare. Shame on those drivers for polluting the street with noise!

Twenty drummers ended their performance on one tight note. The façades busied themselves with echoing applause.

As I fell asleep that night, I kept thinking about the fans—the parents in the thresholds and their kids holding their cool little coffee-can-sized drums.

***

Next morning: still coughing up essence of bourgeois chair leg. Someone was spray-painting a mural on the façade of an art foundation across from my hotel. I had already started a collection of mural photos from previous walks in Montevideo—Batman with a bare, protruding gut; Jesus in tighty-whities; fish with opposable thumbs. The streets were speaking. I kept listening.

I wondered what statement the rusty Studebakers and Morrises along the curb were making. Despite contributing to the city's sooty air, the cars must have been tickling a particular aesthetic fancy. Some were junked, and were somehow entitled to parking spots as their final resting places, where they oxidized in peace: a charming respect for the elderly. It was as if removing them would be an act of vandalism.

Manicured plazas line the city's main avenue, 18 de Julio, at conveniently regular intervals, natural meeting points of which Montevideans take advantage. Young couples nuzzling foreheads, mothers nursing al fresco, a trio in soccer jerseys sharing a gourd of bitter yerba maté tea on a park bench. Texting remained a rare sight.

At this early hour, the drummers had swapped out their instruments for gourds and hot water–filled thermoses as they walked into bakeries or music stores. But their presence lingered. Several murals featured depictions of candombe drumming, past and present. When I asked a tailor if any *cuerdas* perform in the narrow streets near his Ciudad Vieja storefront, he dropped his scissors, fetched his own drum that he stores in his shop, and dove into an excited description—half verbal, half manual—of his own *cuerda*, all while someone's pants lay on the table charmingly unhemmed.

I passed a couple piles of ashes near the curb, evidence of recent *cuerda* activity. Back in the States, street drummers—just like roadside car carcasses—would usually be viewed as quality-of-life violations (especially when adding in the public alcohol consumption). I remained intrigued at the *cuerda's* acceptance in Montevidean society.

It would be the frequency of murals, bustling central plazas, and curb-beautifying Studebakers that would begin to cast light on the popularity of the city's public percussion. And perhaps vice versa. There was an undeniable current of social electricity coursing through the streets of Montevideo, streets serving as destinations that help bond neighbors so they feel they live with the city, not just in it. In those streets, *cuerdas*—group efforts themselves—had been born.

***

For the past week, I'd been in taxis blocked by *cuerdas*. I'd walked with *cuerdas* that blocked taxis. But I had yet to experience the music from the drummer's perspective.

I took my first lesson with Tatita Marquez—drummer, composer, and candombe historian—in his studio, located on a stencil-sprinkled block in that apparent contradiction of a neighborhood, middle-class Pocitos. He had painted the walls of his studio in alternating colors, reminding me of hues for shag rugs—lime green, Muppet orange. A thicket of drums and mixing boards surrounded us.

Since his college years, he has been fusing candombe with electronic and other forms of music, and has toured on three continents. But for our lesson, he introduced me to the basic street-drumming patterns he grew up with, on all three candombe drums, the *chico*, *repique*, and *piano*—small, medium, and large, respectively. His head shaven, he was all muscle and passion poking out from a tank top. "We start with wood," he said, referring to candombe's characteristic strike of the stick on the drum shell.

The accents took a crisp departure from the downbeat-intensive grooves of my days as a drummer in a punk 'n' roll band some years ago. And I had never used the candombe configuration—one stick and one hand. But what slowly blossomed was an interlocking rhythm between our drums, hitting the same pleasure receptors as when biting into a complex yet well-balanced dish. Each flavor—or rhythm—complements the others in some predetermined, perfected way, the combination of which is greater than the sum of its parts.

The rhythm formed a lively dialog, a food group for social animals. Fittingly, the drum parades during Carnival are called *llamadas*, or calls, as in calling neighbors to join the parade when it passes by.

***

Many of them can't stand up by themselves. I'm talking about yerba maté gourds. Since Mother Nature rarely offers us fruit with flat surfaces, the gourds, when dried

"The rhythm formed a lively dialog, a food group for social animals."

and fashioned into teacups, need little legs sewn onto them to keep them from falling over. Most Uruguayans have still not forsaken the old-school gourd—kind of like a handheld Studebaker—for something requiring less maintenance.

As I watched the Uruguayans clutching their maté paraphernalia while they climbed into buses, hung out in the city's plazas, or sat in the thresholds of crumbling colonial tenements, it became clear that the awkward portability of the thermos-and-gourd routine should not be mistaken for accessories to a fast-lane lifestyle. The gear is designed to allow the drinker to share tea outside the house and in the social fabric of the streets. The leisurely passing of the legless gourd from friend to friend in front of a manicured fountain seemed to reveal identity much more than inconvenience.

Only a strong sense of identity could keep a Uruguayan gripping his thermos between

Candombe drum mural in Montevideo

his arm and chest while dancing in front of a *cuerda*. The first time I saw this, the metaphorical implications were inescapable: his arm out as if holding a partner, giving the image of a dancing couple, man and thermos, spinning together.

By my last drum lesson, the effect of identity had colored the mood more than the walls of Tatita's studio. He taught me three

> "As if refusing to acknowledge that the weekend is ending, Sunday nights are the biggest for *cuerdas*."

different but related rhythms that have originated in three neighborhoods. The districts—Barrio Sur, Palermo, Cordon—are close to one another; in a half-hour walk, you could hit them all. But each rhythm has its own feel: the accelerated speed in Cordon, the extra accent on the *chico* in Palermo. Terroir for music.

Tatita was born in Palermo, a neighborhood where Afro-Uruguayans started marching candombe drums through the streets in the 1940s. Apparently, no womb within earshot has been immune to the tug of rhythms that eventually leaped over the walls of racism. I asked the thirty-five-year-old Tatita how long he has been playing; with a confident nod, he answered, "thirty-five years." Mental picture drawn: a tyke-sized drum strapped onto a tyke-sized Tatita.

The grownup Tatita related stories of how the military dictatorship, from 1973 to 1984, would throw someone in jail for playing drums in the streets, except during a few allowed fiestas. With the return of street drumming, the dialog of candombe rhythms is changing, as all living languages do. Some groups are starting to play different *claves*, or basic rhythm keys. "People prefer the new breaks," he commented. He switched to English, for emphasis, and added, "Some think their candombe died, but it is the evolution of candombe."

If it weren't for evolution, we would have neither tango nor candombe. Both styles find common roots in African rhythms, but diverged over a century ago. Tango acquired European instrumentation and melodies, and candombe simplified the *clave* while becoming the percussive backbone of many Uruguayan jazz and rock recordings.

He offered me a gourd filled to the top with loose tea. The metal straw resembled a little oboe reed, preventing the water from being slurped, thus keeping it hot. After one sip, my head felt like a giant tea bag, stuffed with freshly mowed grass and oregano, that had been dunked in a bucket of hot water. Tatita snickered, not the laughing-with-you kind.

I hesitated. He returned to the same didactic seriousness as when teaching me how to spread my fingers to strike a bass note on the *piano*. "You have to finish it," he said.

Some facets of Uruguayan identity are more easily understood than others.

***

Sundays are usually calm in Latin America. Not in Montevideo. Starting at sunrise, the city's largest street market bursts with musty Carlos Gardel LPs, machetes, albino puppies, tomatoes, thermos-clenching elbows. By late afternoon, the restaurant *parrilladas* will have seared over a ton of steak. As if refusing to acknowledge that the weekend is ending, Sunday nights are the biggest for *cuerdas*.

One of the most popular is La Melaza, an all-female group. While almost every *cuerda* has at least a few women, the ratio still tips heavily in the direction of men, hence the formation of La Melaza (they do, however, encourage male drummers to join them the last week each month).

How large is La Melaza? When I approached the dead end where the drums sat around a fire, I asked a young member crouching in comfy sweatpants, her fingers taped up. "Maybe forty this time," she said, "but it depends on who shows up. You can always count the drums."

When the group lined up and began marching, I became part of a throng following the drummers. The fans outnumbered the drummers two to one. I ran into Lalo, who corrected me when he spotted me walking behind the *cuerda*. Walking? That's a no-no. "Step like this," Lalo commanded, stomping on the quarter notes, so that we all formed one inseparable gust of humanity, together with the thermos dancers, the synchronized hands slapping *chico* drums, and the occasional fan squatting and pissing in the middle of the street.

Cartons of wine made from tannat, a grape common in Uruguayan wineries, made

A cuerda marching in Montevideo

their way around. I'm sure there is an interesting story that explains why candombe drums are usually played with just one stick, but a few drummers demonstrated another incentive: you can keep the beat with the stick and still grab a swig from the carton when it comes by.

Uruguayan musician Hugo Fattoruso kicks off the first track of his jazz-candombe album *Emotivo* with a spirited narration of his country's candombe heritage, celebrating candombe's "*calor de piel*," or heat of the skin, which can conveniently refer to the drumhead, the hands, or both. As I fielded a carton of tannat, the buildings locked in said warmth like a blanket, wrapping it around me, around the drummers, around the residents dancing on the balconies. Coming from the often fragmented social landscape of New York, I was overwhelmed, but also enchanted—comfortably adrift in a people connected to each other, a people connected to a city. A city where drums contribute to the quality of life.

***

The week before I had arrived in Montevideo, I met a Uruguayan student outside a sausage cart in Panama City. "I've been living in Panama for three years now, but I still hear the drums in my head every Sunday night," he remarked. A rather romantic statement, I thought. And one that resurfaced when I was in a taxi going to the airport for my departure from Uruguay. The driver handed me some crackers, the most humble of the many edible offerings the Uruguayans had shared with me. Then I realized what I was doing. I was chewing in the rhythm of the *clave*.

Photos courtesy of Darrin DuFord
This story previously appeared on PerceptiveTravel.com

The Audacity of Children

by Heidi Swedberg

There was usually a pot of beans, rice, and some kind of stew on the stove at the Global Family Philanthropy Home (an orphanage) in Les Cayes, Haiti. Smells of cooking filled the small concrete building. The languid tropical-style flow of women cooking and cleaning: hypnotic. The air flowing through the back door cooled the sheltered stoop where big basins of laundry were washed by hand. It was a lovely spot to gaze at the soft layers of green and grey that is the Haitian landscape. Strata of pale corn, tall breadfruit trees, soft low grasses, broad banana fields, and whispering cane made a horizontal quilt beneath grey clouds. As rain landed on tin roofs and fresh concrete, I took a break to find perspective, savoring the taste of chilled lager. From there you could see the beauty but not the difficulty of life in Haiti. At that moment, forgotten were the oppressive smell of diesel smoke, the hardship of living in tents and shacks, and the poverty.

The children's main meal was taken around two o'clock in the afternoon. Two long, hand-built tables were set with large tin plates brimming with food. The kids sat down to their meal and ate for nearly a full hour every day. They filled their dear mouths and bellies determinedly. Twenty-odd unrelated siblings seated side-by-side on wobbly wooden chairs would talk, laugh, bicker, cry, and work out problems amongst themselves. They dined in the main room, a wall of ukuleles alongside them. Their lives lived out in that small, safe space.

We sixteen volunteers had arrived earlier that day in the rain via the back of an open pickup truck, carrying with us the ukuleles so I could teach the kids how to play. When we pulled into the grounds of the Home, we were greeted with shrieks of elation. Ten or more kids bounced out, arms wide, full of smiles and hugs.

A crowd of seven-year-old boys encircled me with chants of "gee-tar! gee-tar!" They would not stop until the ukuleles were pulled down from the wall, tuned, and passed out. One-hundred-degree heat would not keep their little bodies from vying for a spot on my lap. Like all kids they wanted attention, they wanted it all, and they wanted it IMMEDIATELY! They had the same audacity as children all around the world. Curiosity and enthusiasm burst from them. Their eyes had yet to confront the hopelessness of poverty and despair.

I was worried that my lack of French or Creole would curtail my ability to teach, but I had underestimated the agility of young minds. Before I could struggle through my few words of explanation, the little mimics would speed ahead, learning by imitation. I indicated the fingering for chords "C" and "F," and that gave them all they needed to know.

They shouted, "*Les Rouges! Yon sèl, de, twa, kat. Changer les vertes . . . yon sèl, de, twa, kat! Les Rouges . . .*" (which means "Red! One, two, three, four. Change to green . . . one, two, three, four! Red . . .").

Thus we played every French children's song I could think of, all three of the Haitian songs I had come to know, and Bob Marley's greatest hits. "Sur le pont d'Avignon" was a two-chord favorite. We would all play and dance around with that one. A dozen small children—without a care in the world—bowed and curtseyed and laughed. After about half-an-hour they would know they were done, hand back the instruments and wander away.

I learned one great song while I was in Haiti: a call and response song, "Ti Poulette." When wandering around, being an obvious outsider attracting a crowd of skeptical stares, I would smile at the curious and start a verse. And the crowd would immediately laugh and sing the next, and I would sing the response, "Wi Wa!" Suddenly strangers were friends.

The climate was so wet and hot it became apparent that the cardboard cases in which the instruments were kept would not last and that the instruments I had brought were in danger of being destroyed by persistent flooding. Thankfully, I had also brought a sewing project related to the chicken houses being built at the Home, so I taught the kids and adults how to make little hand-sewn chicks.

There was an empty wall on which I was asked to paint a mural. That's when it all came together. I painted a fat yellow chick with a red ukulele, and two little chicks beside her. I also painted the chorus to a song, as well as the chord diagrams for the song and a few others (the C chord family and relative minor family). The ukes were hung on the wall, and there it was: a lesson, a song, a mural, an illustration, and a storage place!

We left in the pickup truck at about five o'clock that evening. It was still raining. The kids waved goodbye. Some cried, though we assured them we would return the next day and the rest of the week. Our time there was shorter than any of us cared to acknowledge. We waved goodbye and back the children went into the shelter of the Home, to dormitories of metal bunk beds and clean white sheets, to their dreams, and to the rest of their childhoods.

Scan to Listen
or visit
www.sombk.co/v1/61

"Wi Wa"
by Heidi Swedberg

"Wi Wa" used with permission from Heidi Swedberg and BMI

Fruit

by Karina Borowicz

Screened by cedar trees
a woman is singing
in the small garden behind
the stone library
bare knees just visible
folded over the granite bench

no one who passes can know
who this voice belongs to
as it vines around
the iron framework of a song

an utterance with no future
no past only the now
of a pulsing throat

no one recognizes the words
just the ripeness of vowels
that give weight and a burst
of sweetness to what would have been
a fruitless day

Metronome

by Tracie Renee Amirante Padal

Your first breath
fades to a grand pause: the diminuendo of your weak cry
heralds a swift shift of tone and tempo in the delivery room.
The problem, they say, is your heart. Swaddled in wires
and the unnatural hush of paralytic drugs, you disappear
through a door I cannot see beyond, into a sterile chamber
busy with the silver singing of surgical instruments.
Your first lullabies are the rise and fall of voices in the hall,
keeping time against the coded blips and measured ticks
of monitors counting your breath. For weeks after,
the ventilator's white noise wheeze lulls you to sleep,
and all I can do is listen, wanting more for you
than the nervous tremelo of a restless dream.

I want to see you grow. I want you to grow up, dancing.
My touch does little to ease your sighs, but I want you to know
that there is more to this life than the hospital's mechanical hum
and the syncopated clang of the vitals cart. I want you to know
the sunrise preludes of robins, the honeyed harmonies of strummed guitars
and muffled melody of winter snow. Christmas morning, I brush dust
off an old LP and let it spin on the record player. The needle nudges
soft secrets from vinyl grooves, and your small fists unfurl
to reach up and beg for more. I want you to keep reaching, to never stop—
so I play it again. You drum the tabletop with jazz hands. Week by week and
song by song, the tight line of stitches over your breastbone
fades to a muted scar and your heart finds its rhythm:
a metronome of hope.

Music Making 1

by Vinesh Rajpaul

A young girl takes her cello lesson in the Plaza Estado del Vaticano, Buenos Aires.

Swans

by Nancy Gustafson

In a circle of light
    like moonlight on water,
        wearing white satin
            she walked to center stage.
                The audience hushed.
Cradling her cello with graceful arms
    she drew the bow across the strings
        and Saint-Saëns' "Le Cygne" filled the hall
        Inspiriting
            every soul.

In the candles' glow
    as gentle as twilight,
        gowned in white satin
            she stood at the altar.
                The congregation hushed.
Encircling him with tender arms
    she drew her husband to her life
        with promises rising like incense
        Singing
            of love and sacrifice.

In diffuse shadows
    from a pale milky moon
        she cradled her daughter
            like a cygnet beneath feathered wings.
                The crying baby hushed.

Scan to Listen
or visit
www.sombk.co/v1/66

The author's reading
of the poem

Enfolding her in down-soft arms
    she drew the infant to her heart
        tracing her brows, her cheeks, her lips
          Humming
            "Le Cygne," a gift surrendered.

In rays of sunshine
    more brilliant than moonlight
        her family grew in beauty,
          an orchestrated harmony.
          In the interlude
dreams of concertos and white satin gowns
    flew like winter swans
        through a veil of clouds
          Receding
            from sight over restless waters.

In a circle of light
    like moonlight on water,
        wearing white satin
          her daughter walked to center stage.
          The audience hushed.
She drew the bow across the cello's strings.
    "Le Cygne's" legato infused the air,
        resonant with her mother's dream
          Rippling
            feathers on peaceful waters.

Scan to Listen
or visit
www.sombk.co/v1/67a

"Le Cygne"
performed by
Annete Di Giosia,
the author's sister

Scan to Listen
or visit
www.sombk.co/v1/67b

The story
behind the poem

An earlier version of this poem was published in A Book of the Year 2000 *from the Poetry Society of Texas*

Gluzman Sees a Ghost

by Craig Baker

When they first handed world-class Soviet-Israeli violinist Vadim Gluzman the instrument he plays today, he says he had the "distinct feeling" that he was being watched. This is no ordinary violin, mind you, so it would make sense that a number of people were looking on. But this feeling was different, supernatural even.

Gluzman's violin is more than just a spectacular musical instrument. In fact, the instrument he plays is as much a work of art as any of the thousands of concertos intoned across its tender strings. A treasure of the musical world, the rare violin is worth millions of dollars—literally more than its weight in gold—and it features a price tag that is higher than any classical musician alive could afford.

That's because Gluzman's violin was crafted in 1690 by Italian master stringed-instrument maker, Antonio Stradivari, a man widely regarded as the foremost artisan ever to practice his craft. It is a violin so unique that it has a title known by connoisseurs the world over: they call it the "Ex-Auer." The instrument is so-called for its former owner, Leopold Auer, who was a Hungarian musician and educator who Gluzman says, "set the cornerstone for Russian violin school" in the late nineteenth century. The Ex-Auer changed hands several times before it was acquired by a patron of the Stradivari Society of Chicago in the 1980s, and, seventeen years ago, it was placed reverently in Gluzman's care. It was then, in the halls of the Stradivari Society building in 1997, that Gluzman had the feeling of eyes on his back. "You know sometimes you have that sensation, that sort of discomfort?" he says. "And I turned around and right behind me on the wall was a huge portrait of Auer staring at me—that was the spookiest thing I have ever experienced in my life." Then he laughs.

Still, contrary to what you might believe, Gluzman says that he did not have an instant connection with the priceless violin, despite the surreal circumstances surrounding the transfer of the rare instrument into his keep. "It's just not that easy to play an instrument like that," Gluzman explains. Every violin, he says, has its own personality: its own likes, dislikes, and preferences. And so it took some time for the new owner to learn how the instrument responded to him. But, once he developed a feel for the classic violin, Gluzman says, "the sensation was incredible—suddenly I could do things that I didn't even dream of before."

Gluzman first began playing music at the age of seven while living with his parents—both music teachers—in the Soviet Union. Though he was just looking for their attention at first, when he asked to begin his education in music, his parents marched him directly to the local conservatory, where he underwent a rigorous series of tests. His first grade class of seven students was selected from a crop of about a hundred, and he says he was assigned the violin simply because he was "built for it." At the time, though, he had no idea how true this might be.

In 1990, when he was sixteen, Gluzman's family fled the Soviet Union for Israel. Two weeks after their arrival in Jerusalem, the young man's long and distinguished career in music got a jumpstart from a serendipitous encounter with a world-famous Israeli violinist and philanthropist. The boy found his own way to the Jerusalem Music Centre that day and inquired with a receptionist about arranging an audition with founder and headmaster, Isaac Stern. "This," the receptionist told him, "would not be possible." It took months to gain an audience with Stern, and there was a long process involved, and paperwork. Gluzman protested. And protested. Stern, who happened upon the situation by chance, heard the teenaged Gluzman arguing with his employee and offered the boy five minutes to warm up before his one shot at a private audience. After a two-hour

> "Despite a life that has carried him across the world and back countless times, Gluzman still finds himself occasionally lost on stage. . . ."

session that day, Stern gave Gluzman a new violin, a music scholarship, and a ticket to study with him in Tel Aviv.

Gluzman went on to study further at Juilliard and, later, to perform as a soloist with nearly every orchestra of any renown across the globe—from the Seoul and London Philharmonics to the Philadelphia and Chicago Symphony Orchestras—and to live a jet-setting dream far beyond the imagination of that young Soviet-born boy turned Israeli émigré.

Despite a life that has carried him across the world and back countless times, Gluzman still finds himself occasionally lost on stage, ever in search of those brief moments when the boundary between man and instrument disappears. "When there is no more me and it," he says, "when we become one and it's just my voice, that's very special." And it feels—and sounds—like music.

This story previously appeared in the Arizona Jewish Post

Teaching Mozart in Stone Mountain Prison

by Karen Paul Holmes

I didn't know what crimes they committed,
didn't want to: those twelve guys glaring at me,
wondering what I had in store.

No female had taught there before
so I wore a calf-length, shapeless dress,
no makeup, tortoise-shell glasses instead of contacts.

Twice a week, iron gates banged behind me,
paperwork shuffled, an armed guard took me down
a warren of halls. He stationed himself by my door.

I needn't have worried—soon knew, just as told,
if one prisoner caused trouble, he'd be jumped
by the others grateful for the chance of a college degree.

This was music appreciation. None knew the classics,
but one had played *William Tell Overture* in band.
All began to embrace opera, symphony, sonata—

I think the music transported them, comforted
even as they struggled to study in noisy rows of bunks.
One evaluation stays with me thirty years later,

"Thanks be to God for blessing us with Mrs. Holmes."
But I felt blessed early in the semester:
We arrived at Mozart Piano Concerto Number 21.

Their books covered just the first movement, yet
I left the record playing into the second, saying,
"You've got to hear a bit of the andante."

Muted violins conjured the ethereal melody while
repeated notes in the violas mesmerized.
After the pianist took up the solo for several bars,

I reached out to lift the needle . . . Twelve students
—no longer thief, mugger, murderer—
sang out in unison, "No, leave it on!"

This poem was first published in POEM Literary Magazine *(Huntsville, Alabama)*

Exodus

by Julia Price

Scan to Listen

or visit
www.sombk.co/v1/73

"Exodus"
by Julia Price

"Exodus" is an original piece that explores the meaning and interpretations of freedom, time, and symbolism. The opening words borrow from a passage in the Bible that remains significant to religious traditions around the globe—the "Lords Prayer." The words are spoken in a self-reflective manner, almost as an initiation into a time, or "realm" that is perhaps fixed within the global, human memory. Words, in theory, leave marks on us, meaning once spoken the sounds and meanings stain us with their "wisdom" or their "curse." These particular words from the "Lords Prayer" seem to not only play on a spiritual theme, but when considered creatively, they entertain concepts of change and freedom. I created each sound as a symbol, deliberately introducing a theme as a foundation. This theme is a reoccurring pattern that stabilizes the song—the melody—while the other spontaneous patterns that occur compositionally play on the statement of how the urge and instinctual lust for change and materialization serve us as a way to access who we are. It seems that no matter who we are, change is meant to re-invite the theme of total purpose back into the human experience, which of course ultimately binds us all—no matter who or what our identities instruct us to be. But beyond tradition, this departure (or "Exodus") could expedite our perceptions of ourselves, and of the world around us. Each unique experience could perhaps be borrowed from a common source, and just as it branches out, chaotically or formidably, the changes just happen so that eventually we are lead, successfully, back into our constancy.

Beyond the Sand:
A story of loss, despair, and the healing power of rock music

by Maria Edible

"The first time I cut myself was soon after my father died," my friend Joe tells me, his voice competing with waves climbing the shore. "It was with the scissors he used to trim his beard." I look down, staring at a sleepy bee clinging to the wooden table. Everything is black, except for a small lantern and the lemon-slivered moon dangling overhead.

"I felt like I deserved to bleed."

We're in Roatán, Honduras, on a group vacation with friends. Everyone is here to unwind, sunbathe, snorkel. The island welcomes us with colors—cascading parapets of green, a surfeit of blue as far as the eye can see. When we arrive, the warm air wafts over us in rolling swells. Our house is on a hill, its back deck encircled by massive palm trees, heavy with coconuts (soon to be introduced to our bottle of rum). Serpentine paths lead to undisclosed locations and we're all electric with wanderlust.

Joe is taking a break from his job as a marketing director for a musical equipment distribution company. He has also stepped away from The You Rock Foundation, an organization he founded to combat depression and suicide through intimate interviews with musicians. Joe's involvement with You Rock comes from a personal place; most of his life, he has battled depression—

debilitating, self-destructive, merciless depression. During the lowest times, he turned to music and found an enduring source of support, which he now shares with struggling fans.

We're splitting a Salva Vida (a local *cerveza*) at our private beach, just seconds away from our property. Above us, past the straw umbrella, is an expanse of nothing stretching to infinity. There's a welcome sense of isolation, an individual claim to this secluded spot, a pushpin on a great map.

Although I've known Joe for over four years, he's a sketch to me, lines upon white paper. I know there's so much more and I'm ready to hear his story.

Joe starts at the beginning, from the days of elementary school play stardom and the bright eyes of a social, personable kid. There was a loving, tight-knit family with three siblings and a cluster of smiling childhood portraits. At some point in middle school, his classmates' insensitive words began to sting and he withdrew, his self-worth diminishing daily. He became introverted and angry. "You know when you see a car driving in front of you with family stickers—a mom, a dad, a daughter, a son, and a dog? I feel like if my family had those stickers they'd all be happy, white silhouettes, and then there'd be one crushed, distorted black one for me," Joe tells me, shadows marching on his face.

He tries to explain what it's like to be lost in the haze of depression. "It's a fucking trickster, a liar," Joe says. "You tell yourself all these terrible things and it doesn't matter how many times someone tells you you're loved and appreciated." He looks at me solemnly. "You're blind, deaf, and dumb to it all." Shortly after his sixteenth birthday, Joe's father died in a car crash, minutes away from home. He felt it all night, an unexplainable paranoia, a desire to call him. When Joe woke up the next day and heard voices, he already knew what happened. "I took a bat and went up the hill to a tree and smashed the bat against the tree until I was exhausted and the bat was broken," he tells me, slowly.

That very same day, Joe sought out music for relief. He didn't have the ability to put his emotions into words, so he turned to an industrial rock band called Nine Inch Nails. Quarantined in his basement, he heard "Something I Can Never Have" and "A Warm Place" (an instrumental piece) and found temporary solace, a source of vicarious expression. Unknown to him then, on the opposite side of the computer desk, his brother lay curled up in the fetal position, quietly listening along.

"When my dad died, it was a confirmation for me that I didn't deserve any love," Joe recalls. After the accident, he felt a tremendous amount of anger. There was a profound hostility toward religion and being forced to attend church and worship a God that betrayed him. Mainly, there was a torrent of rage directed inward: guilt for not

Joseph Penola, Founder of The You Rock Foundation

listening to his intuition the night of his father's death and not picking up the phone to call him.

"I was the last person in my family to see him alive, and I was an asshole to him," Joe tells me as he remembers that morning. His dad dropped him off at school and told him to "make it a great day," his signature phrase of encouragement. Joe said nothing and slammed the door, a typical act of teenage acidity that would resonate with him for many years.

There's a sudden growling behind me. My breath catches and I spin, quickly. It's a yellow Lab, eyeing us distrustfully, emitting bark after hostile bark. Joe calls to him but he scampers away, excitedly yelping to alert his owner (the groundskeeper of our vacation house).

I turn my attention back to the story. About two years after his father's death, Joe recounts skipping his senior prom and going straight to the afterparty. Recovering from a breakup, he was mired in a circuit of self-loathing. The synergy of loss and rejection led him to ingest a mind-boggling mixture of alcohol, MDMA, and cocaine. Later, Joe woke up in a shower, placed there by a friend concerned by his unresponsive state.

I'm stirred by this and my narrow view of suicide. After all, the act is not merely defined by an empty bottle of pills or a razor piercing skin and inching toward a vein. It's a downbeat mindset, a mental low that compels someone to engage in various forms of self-destructive behavior.

That wasn't the only time for Joe. "I walked into the ocean wanting to drown," he says, eyes fixed on the dark space beyond the sand. It's my first time hearing my friend admit that he has tried to kill himself. I don't know how to react, so I don't. "I got really close, until there was water in my lungs and didn't stop until I was gasping for air, struggling to live," he adds.

After the suicide attempts, which didn't register as such at the time, Joe went on to cut himself for the sake of the sensation and the ability to control his pain in some small way. Often, the urge came instantaneously. While moving out of an apartment he could no longer afford, Joe broke a mirror, leaving shards all over the floor. He picked one up and forcefully dug it into one shoulder blade, followed by the other. "It felt good—the sensation of piercing my skin with the glass, seeing myself bleed," he recalls.

Despite being surrounded by family and friends, Joe continued to feel alone, invisible, unloved. "Nothing is as debilitating as the loneliness," he says as we start the short walk back to the house. His voice is calm, soothing in timbre, and I suddenly realize how tired I am. "It's not being able to imagine a future," Joe tells me and walks ahead, his sneakers scraping along the rocky path.

***

The next day, our friends discover a new beach to explore, a short hike away from our property. I join Joe for our third session of the Insanity workout, ending up in an immobile, sweaty pile on the deck. Afterward, we grab our snorkeling gear and set out to find our group.

I follow Joe up a narrow, hillside path barely discernible from below. A refreshing breeze welcomes us into a green hallway, tall pillars of grass slow dancing to the rhythm of the wind. There is evidence of strange activity all around us—a large hole dug by some creature, a constant shuffling in the shrubs on both sides, the melodic discourse of unfamiliar birds. Tiny slivers of leaves move in rows underfoot, carried by industrious leafcutter ants. There's a sense of induction, and I feel like an inactive participant, a still figure in this tableau of swirling island life.

We arrive at a fence with a slender opening and Joe pulls it toward him so I can slip through. I look closer at his left bicep and there they are—a series of white, horizontal lines, not blatant but easily distinguishable. He shows me his other arm, which has a thicker, more pronounced scar that starts at the wrist and flows into a nautilus shell tattoo, a personal representation of *The*

Downward Spiral album by Nine Inch Nails. This one is different—it was done right along the vein. "I was not expecting to kill myself there but I was hoping I would get close," he tells me under the midday blaze.

During the time that I have been friends with Joe, his love for Nine Inch Nails was common knowledge. Still, I never realized how much each word, each riff really meant to him. "Trent Reznor saved my life," Joe tells me. He listened to *The Downward Spiral* over and over again. "It was such a relief to know this person might feel like I do. He could put words to things I was struggling not only to say out loud but to even think, admit to myself," Joe says, navigating the winding path to the water. "I could sing along. I could scream along. All of a sudden, that dam I had built up in myself was broken, flooding out." In his despondent state, Joe relied heavily on three bands: the aforementioned Nine Inch Nails, Tool, and Deftones. The rock triumvirate has remained at the top of his list to this day.

A chorus of familiar voices grows in volume as we pass a broad thicket of bamboo, a creaking emanating from within. Exotic yellow fruit resembling diminutive peppers line the ground, sweetly rotting under swarms of ants.

For Joe, music granted permission to feel emotions that would normally remain hidden, ignored, denied. "It's the same as reading a beautiful passage in a book or a piece of poetry that touches some intangible part of you," Joe tells me, inspecting the fallen fruit, whose thick, syrupy smell lingers in the air.

I ask Joe if he thinks turbulent lyrics can amplify anger or worse. He concedes that aside from the customary relief, there were times his fury was accelerated. Still, Joe maintains that

"For Joe, music granted permission to feel emotions that would normally remain hidden, ignored, denied."

music shouldn't be blamed for an act of violence, against oneself or another. "It just brings out whatever is already in you."

When we arrive at the miniature beach, our crew is reduced to a series of protruding snorkels. The shore is composed of elaborate rock formations, shaped by the artistry of steadfast water erosion. Groups of skinny cacti hang off the edges, their bodies pinched like sausages in a butcher shop. I notice a black and white iguana (or Michael Jackson, as this breed was affectionately referred to by a local) drowsing on a boulder, its scaly back glimmering in the light. My eyes drift momentarily, and when they return, it's gone.

I shimmy into my fins and waddle awkwardly into the water. Gripping the snorkel with my teeth, I dive in. The sounds of the island disappear and I can hear only the laborious suction of my own breath. Rows of gaudy fish flutter in and out of cavernous coral, ignoring my presence. Several feet away, Joe is distracted by a crumpled pile of corroded metal, a reputed shipwreck. I wave at him, unable to shake the image of his suicide attempt, a determined walk into the incomprehensible depths.

Eventually, I miss the comfort of unrestrained breathing and come up. I find Joe sitting solo in a grotto, incoming waves crashing against its walls.

"Come on," he says, beckoning for me to join him on top of an elevated rock. I step up and immediately fall backwards as I take a punch from an irate barricade of water.

"This is amazing, you have to see this view," Joe encourages, offering his hand. I lunge forward in another attempt and am slammed back by a fizz of white and blue. Disheartened,

"The idea for You Rock came from Joe's personal experience—he wanted to help people like him . . ."

I sit down on a flat stone slimed with algae. The grotto's inner landscape has a lunar quality, its pockmarked sides dotted with delicate pockets of light.

Soon, Joe sidles up next to me. I ask him the one question I've been holding back—whether he's overcome his depression. I understand that this might not elicit the answer I hope to hear.

"No," he replies, in a way that suggests he has come to terms with that notion. "Anyone that says depression is something

you conquer or defeat for life is lying or living in a fantasy. It's especially true if there's a traumatic trigger involved like death or abuse." Joe runs his fingers through the rushing water, looking toward the source of the waves, somewhere outside the grotto's opening. "You just learn how to manage it, and music is one of the many tools that helps me," he says.

Whether Joe's experience is typical or not, the response is practical, realistic. After all, there are many afflictions that permanently anchor themselves, and perhaps depression is no different. Proper regulation can keep them nipping at our heels, rather than hanging onerously around our necks. I look at Joe and smile. He'll be all right.

***

The morning sun won't let me sleep past seven, so I join it and drink my coffee on the balcony. There isn't a single person in sight, just an avalanche of green sweeping down the hillside, encompassing leaves of every shade and shape. A turkey vulture soars by effortlessly, swooping and rising again in one swift motion. It's an odd perception—being confronted with the absence of humanity—one of apocalyptic tranquility.

A car picks us up and takes us to the ferry for Little French Key, an island resort several miles away. After a boisterous encounter with a troop of capuchin and spider monkeys (who enthusiastically climbed Joe's face), he and I settle down on a waterlogged bench next to the bar, cherry-topped piña coladas in tow. The resort offers multiple options for parking your drink, whether it's a straw umbrella stand or a partially submerged chaise lounge, all distributed throughout the aquamarine seawater. The rich smell of sunblock clings to my nostrils, a comforting reminder vis-à-vis the scorching rays.

The idea for You Rock came from Joe's personal experience—he wanted to help people like him, those who could barely get through the day. His professional connections provided the starting point to get musicians on board to tell their stories. "No one is immune from depression; financial success, fame—none of that inoculates you," Joe says, taking a sip of his rapidly melting drink.

Currently staffed by volunteers, You Rock functions by recording interviews with music artists who share their experiences, struggles, and most importantly, their recovery. The videos are then promoted through social media platforms such as Facebook, Instagram, and Twitter to reach their audience, as well as spread awareness and battle stigma.

You Rock has published interviews with Jonathan Davis of Korn, Corey Taylor of Slipknot and Stone Sour, Ben Weinman of The Dillinger Escape Plan, Jesse Leach of Killswitch Engage, and Chris Robertson of Black Stone Cherry. For Joe, the talks with Jon and Corey were particularly compelling—their songs supported him when he was at rock-bottom. Jon spoke about his experience with depression (which he compared to "a giant lead blanket"), and Corey shared his

"Although You Rock is primarily aimed at those struggling with mental illness, their hope is to reach anyone who needs a boost."

harrowing experience of ending up in a hospital after swallowing a handful of pills. Both rock stars proffered advice on how to plow through the crushing despair and insisted that the future is far from bleak.

Joe is now supine on the bench, his eyes obscured by a pair of Ray-Bans, oblivious to the striped, fingernail-sized fish darting in and out of the wooden slats. The sky is punctuated by an aggressive blur of white and gold, and every few minutes, there's a welcome breeze, a toss of good fortune, and the consuming heat is subdued, if only for a brief moment.

In an upbeat tone, he emphasizes the importance of broadcasting artist testimonials to complement their music. For legions of fans, recording artists reside on a pedestal, superficially steeping in success and happiness. To see them fall is enlightening, to watch them soar, inspiring. Joe witnessed his favorite musician, Trent Reznor, sink into the pits of depression, no different from himself. When Trent overcame substance abuse and straightened out, it helped Joe push through the most dismal days of his life.

I nod. We often take music for granted. It's a neatly packaged form of amusement, something to provide energizing party soundtracks and trigger impromptu shower concerts. However, we tend to forget that there are artists behind the words, bleeding from the speakers, wringing out years of experiences, trials, and aspirations.

Although You Rock is primarily aimed at those struggling with mental illness, their hope

"Despite the organization's ostensible focus on rock music, Joe has plans to include artists from multiple communities—EDM, hip hop, country, and pop, among others."

is to reach anyone who needs a boost. "Everyone suffers. Through a change in perspective, we want to pull people out of the victim mentality and get them to where they are thriving, lit up by life," Joe says, suddenly animated. He wants to encourage action through diverse means, whether it's music, medication, exercise, nutrition, creative pursuit, or all of the above.

Their slogan, "You matter, you're needed, you rock," is intended as a reminder of one's own importance in order to replace self-deprecation with words of reassurance. "We bully ourselves, we say things to ourselves that we wouldn't say to someone who did us genuine harm," Joe tells me, "and we believe it's true, because we hear it so much, so often." I take a deep breath and think of the voice inside my own head, the one that whispers discouragement almost every single day. He's right. I wouldn't say those things to anyone else.

I feel a pinch on my thigh and catch a glimpse of a guilty-looking, tiny sand crab scurrying underneath the bench. I drum on the planks severely—a warning to any other trespassers.

Despite the organization's ostensible focus on rock music, Joe has plans to include artists from multiple communities—EDM, hip hop, country, and pop, among others. Eventually, he wants to bring You Rock to every major music festival in order to interview performers, and more importantly, fans.

I tell Joe that I previously scrolled through the comments for his YouTube videos, which were uncharacteristically positive in the days of ubiquitous online trolling. Many viewers were brought to tears, empowered, compelled to get out of bed. Hearing feedback makes it all worth it for Joe. "I lose sight of the effect it has because I am not dealing with these people face to face. I get teary-eyed when I read that stuff," he admits, with a chord of conciliation.

As gratifying as the positive responses can be, the urgent emails have taken an immense toll on Joe. He receives messages from individuals who claim to be clutching a bottle of pills, a razor. His voice tinged with a note of regret, Joe tells me he desperately wants to offer consolation but can't due to legal reasons. Although he redirects them to trained personnel, the emotional burden of the exchange lingers long after. We both turn our heads as a tan woman floats by on an inflatable tube the color of bubble gum. A duo of black butterflies, wings dipped in gold, zoom past her, tumbling in the air so haphazardly it's impossible to tell who is the pursued. Buoyant pop music drifts over from yet another bar, just a short swim away, a bizarre soundtrack to such a heavy conversation.

I surmise that spearheading You Rock has had a healing effect on Joe and he agrees, qualifying it as yet another tool to assist in his own mental battle. Although he no longer needs songs to speak for him, he can still relate. "There is still so much guilt and regret connected with my past self, the one that used to punch holes through walls, put his head through windows," Joe tells me. "I need to learn to have compassion for him. I need to hear everything I tell You Rock's audience."

Perhaps that's what makes the organization so driven—a creative director who knows what it feels like to crawl through life.

It's lunchtime and Joe sits up, sluggish from the momentary repose. The water is cool like silk and we glide away, leaving the bench vacant save for its minuscule crustacean residents.

Joe snorkeling in Roatán

***

The rest of the week is spent swimming, drinking, playing board games, and laughing. We make friends with a local cat, a veritable badass, with vertical wall-scaling skills and a proclivity for lizard hunting. Joe seems happy, with very little indication of the negativity lurking somewhere inside. He tells me he accidentally cut himself a few weeks ago on a broken glass. "I saw it bleeding and it felt good, like a mini relapse," he says, and it sinks in. This is a part of his past, an undeniable truth that he's learned to live with, restrain, maneuver around.

Our final morning is bittersweet. We share one more meal together on the deck as the sun continues its ascent. Desiccated fronds hang limply around the powerful trunk of a palm tree, directly underneath its thriving canopy, life and death existing in unison. They sway their yellowing fingers, as if waving goodbye.

Within a few hours, we board our flight home. To my left, Joe promptly falls asleep. I put on my headphones and brace myself to re-enter the real world. I feel the anxiety rising, the usual tension taking solid shape inside my chest. There's so much that needs to be done, and I don't know if I can handle it all.

Maybe we all have our inner voices that we carry around, some shrieking, others whispering.

It's impossible to evict an established part of your personality, your history. You can only accept it and learn to control it. I acknowledge the ugly noise between my ears that tries to convince me of my ineptitude. And just like that, I tell it to hush and crank up the volume on the radio.

Photos of Joseph Penola by Maria Edible

Corey Taylor of Slipknot, an active supporter of The You Rock Foundation (photo and below video interview used with permission from The You Rock Foundation)

Scan to Watch

or visit
www.sombk.co/v1/83

"Corey Taylor Interview"

Corey Taylor of Slipknot talks
about his experience with
depression

Gentle on My Mind:
My meeting with Glen Campbell

by Peter Gerstenzang

Often, when I see some compilation of music from the 1960s being sold on television—Jefferson Airplane playing against images of dancing headbanded hippies—I can't help but feel I'm not getting the whole picture.

Sure, there was great rock 'n' roll, courtesy of the Kinks, the Rascals, and the Stones. Plus, there was stuff that could only be called rock, sarcastically, by the likes of those acid-damaged doofuses, Iron Butterfly.

But there was another musical side to this tumultuous time—well-written, exquisitely arranged pop that was apolitical and introspective. It was music you and your dad could agree on while he took you out for ice cream on a quiet Sunday. It was music by the Association, Spanky and Our Gang, Donovan.

By the end of the decade, it came from one artist in particular. A man who, it seemed, all the world agreed was great: Glen Campbell.

It started for most of us (those who didn't know Campbell had been an ace session man), with "Gentle on My Mind." When I tell you my father and I bonded over this poetic song, sporting a banjo, it sounds so quaint. It's like the next thing I'm going to tell you about is the day I saw my first horseless carriage. But it was really 1967.

Driving around with Dad, we were both knocked out (people said stuff like that back then) by "Gentle on My Mind," which was John Hartford's composition; it overflowed with free verse, totally original images (who calls their beard a "roughening coal pile"?), and absolutely no mention of the Vietnam War, protest, or drugs. This is probably why the tune, so sweeping and sad, still sounds so good today.

My sister, Jill, joined the Glen Campbell fan club, too. Every few Sundays, you'd see him on *The Smothers Brothers Show*. My dad, Jill, and I sat together on the couch in the playroom, laughing at all the counterculture humor, but really waiting for that Southern '60s anomaly—clean-cut Glen Campbell who had hit after hit, culminating with his masterpiece, "Wichita Lineman."

The tune is about a lonely repairman, standing atop a telephone pole, wishing hopelessly he could be back with the girl he lost and literally loves more than life itself. That Sunday night on the couch, when Campbell finished that Jimmy Webb-written song, there was a lot of throat-clearing and people furtively wiping their eyes—even my dad, who never cried, not even after losing his brother in the War.

Flash forward to 2011. I am a humor writer who sometimes gets lucky and interviews his rock heroes. I get particularly lucky in July and I'm assigned to profile my childhood hero, Glen Campbell. The whole thing is unbearably poignant.

My father has died. My sister is debilitated by a stroke. That should be enough, but no. It's been announced that Campbell has Alzheimer's disease. He's finished his final studio album, *Ghost On the Canvas*, and is promoting it. He will be happy to talk to me about it in New York City. I have talked to almost all the guys I idolize in rock. But, after accepting this assignment, I wonder if, even after speaking with Ray Davies, Paul Weller, and Neil Young, I can handle a hang with Glen Campbell—the guy I use to watch on Sundays, who co-starred in a Western with John freakin' Wayne, who played with everybody from Spector to Sinatra.

Campbell was more than a great guitarist—someone who could play like Buck Owens one minute and Charlie Christian the next. He was, to quote Sinatra's old song, "America to me."

After a sleepless night, I gathered my nervous courage and went. I got to the midtown hotel on time and was met by Bobbie, Campbell's rep, in the lobby. She was a pretty, dark-haired woman, who conveyed both the publicist's upbeat demeanor and that nervous vibe that things could go wrong at any time. I didn't think they would, but her shaky smile added to my building panic. Considering I felt like I was about to repel off of Mt. Rushmore and stare into Thomas Jefferson's face, I didn't need any more reason to be anxious. But being a trained actor, I came off as nonchalant as Peter Fonda in *Easy Rider*. It was time to meet Glen Campbell.

The suite was lovely but not overwhelming. It would have made a small clothes closet for Liberace. Glen's charming,

> "Campbell was more than a great guitarist . . . He was, to quote Sinatra's old song, 'America to me.'"

blonde wife, Kim, came out of the bedroom. Bobbie introduced us. Then Kim said, "Let me go get Glen."

I said, "Great." I could feel my breath starting to come fast and thought I should get into bowing position, but, before I could, out came Mr. Campbell.

Except for some sleep smears on his face, and his sandy hair a bit thinner than the old days, he looked just like Glen Campbell. Actually he was cooler. He had on a blue t-shirt, tight black jeans, and black cowboy boots. He looked like a guy from an alt-country band, which made perfect sense, since he basically invented alternative country.

He said, "Hey!" when we were introduced, in that rural-friendly way, asked for my name, and we shook hands firmly. I had to restrain myself from throwing my arms around him and sobbing, while trying to tell him what he had meant to me growing up, and how much my dad had loved his music. That kind of shit happens when you get older.

I'm glad Kim stayed. I'm also glad that having dealt with people who had brain disorders, I knew how to handle the conversation. At first, it was panic inducing. I'd ask Glen a question about, say, working with The Beach Boys. He'd start to tell me about the sessions, what guitar he'd used, and about twenty words into it, he'd pause for what felt like forever. Then would come the words I was to hear often that afternoon: "What was I saying again?"

As a pot smoker, I was unfazed. This short-term memory loss was just like my being stoned and hungry. I remembered trying to leave my room about six times. And each time, I'd pause and think, "Where was I going again? Oh yeah, right."

Once I knew that this great singer wasn't messing with me, I just applied the principles I'd learned getting high, and we were home free.

Glen told me about working with Spector: "He'd invite anybody in, hand 'em a tambourine and say, 'Go over there.'" And he told me about the time he nearly drowned as a little boy, with his uncle squeezing water out of him and his mama praying to Jesus, "Please don't take him now, Lord!" He talked about the first time he had John Hartford play "Gentle on My Mind" for him: "He was so slow, I thought he'd never get through it." And even though he told me he loved the Paul Westerberg-penned title song of his new album, it was the snatch of another song he sang, that had me surreptitiously wiping away tears.

Three or four times that afternoon, Glen suddenly began to sing "The Moon's a Harsh Mistress." And even though Kim kept saying,

"Honey, that's that old Jimmy Webb song," it didn't matter. And hearing that voice—untouched by time—limn the loss expressed in the song told Glen's whole story . . . and mine, yours, and that of everyone who had reached impossibly high, but still couldn't pull the moon down. If I had just posted Glen singing that song on YouTube, I never would've had to write the piece.

The sun outside our window was slowly starting to arc away from us. Bobbie softly crept up to us and gave me an eye, which gently said, "Wrap it up." Knowing Glen's condition was progressive and had only one end, I had to ask him, "Are you afraid to die? Do you think you're going to heaven?"

He smiled peacefully.

"Yeah, I think so," he said. "I was pretty wild there for a while, but I got straightened out. Especially with my marriage. So, yeah, I think I'm gonna be all right."

I made to leave. But first I had to shake Glen Campbell's hand. He must've felt the love and respect that I had for him, because he reached out and pulled me close and gave me a hug—the kind you give someone you know you'll never see again. Then, since I mentioned I play guitar, he slipped his hand into his jeans pocket and handed me an autographed pick. My throat tightened. I'm sure the light from the sunset must've revealed my glassy eyes. I nodded at Glen. Then Bobbie said she'd take me downstairs.

We said goodbye and left. Bobbie and I just looked at each other in the elevator, silently, which was perfect. Because in that hotel suite, ten flights up, everything important, everything worth saying, had already been said.

This story was originally published by Creative Loafing Charlotte

Lifting Spirits During the Vietnam War
An interview with USO performer, Nancy Stratton

by Anna Wall

I am honored to share the story of my mother, Nancy Stratton, who had one of the most extraordinary, fulfilling, and yet terrifying experiences of a lifetime. Forty-five years ago her Kappa Kappa Gamma sorority-singing group was signed as a United Service Organization (USO) performance act. Nancy and her sorority sisters (Chris, Pam, Linda, and Judi) did three tours over the course of two years during the Vietnam War, entertaining the troops throughout Southeast Asia. From hospital wards to remote firebases and an aircraft carrier, they spread laughter, joy, hope, and love to over 100,000 men and women in all branches of the armed forces. Inspired by her story, I asked her to share some of her experiences in an interview.

Anna Wall (AW): Mom, what was the inspiration behind starting the Kappa Picker Group within your sorority chapter?

Nancy Stratton (NS): Prior to going to college at Colorado State University (CSU), I was invited to a legacy luncheon at the Boulder Kappa House. During the luncheon a group of sorority sisters, the Kappa Pickers, performed, and I was very inspired by their enthusiasm and their whole presentation. So, when I went through rush the following August, I decided that I would pledge Kappa and was hoping that I could be part of their Kappa Picker Group. When I found out they did not have a Kappa Picker Group at CSU, I decided to start one and was elected Song Chairman.

AW: What led you to the USO?

NS: Well, I was watching the Bob Hope Vietnam Christmas Special on TV one evening, and I was so moved by what Mr. Hope was doing that I decided in the back of my mind that maybe we as the Kappa Picker Group could go overseas and entertain the troops like he was. I spent six months researching how the process worked—how the USO selected tours and groups to go overseas and entertain the troops—and I came upon James Sheldon's name. He was the West Coast Hollywood producer of USO shows, so I sent him a letter and introduced our group to him. He wrote back and specified that a touring group could only be five members, and at the time, we had nineteen members of our singing group. We narrowed down the group to five members and sent our biographies and pictures to Mr. Sheldon, who took an interest and decided he would like to audition us . . . if we would pay for his first-class airline ticket from Hollywood to Denver. So, we did, and we auditioned at a Shakey's Pizza Parlor in Fort Collins, Colorado.

AW: So, what was Mr. Sheldon's response when you auditioned for him?

NS: He said, "I believe that you five women would be an outstanding show for our troops." He considered us the all-American girls back home—we represented their sisters and girlfriends, and we were the same age as most of the GIs. Mr. Sheldon signed us on and we were to go on our first tour in the summer of 1970.

AW: Did any of you have any professional experience singing or performing?

NS: We did not. We were all shower singers [*laughter*]. No, and that was the uniqueness of our show. Our music was a combination of bluegrass and a jug band—just fun-loving music. Our instruments consisted of a bass—made out of a washtub with a broom handle and gut string—tambourines, maracas, banjos, and guitars. We played the washboard, the spoons, we played the jug, and the highlight of our show was always when we pulled out five kazoos. We were a unique show and had no experience. But, we had two blondes, a redhead, and two brunettes, and that's pretty much all we needed to walk on stage overseas.

AW: That must have been so exciting as five eighteen-year-old girls. What happened next?

NS: We were given our itinerary for our first tour, which was called the Hardship Tour. We were to perform in the hospitals where the

> "Just to see the wounded soldiers being inspired and happy in the moment—that we were taking their minds off of their pain and suffering—was wonderful."

war victims were sent. We went to Japan, Korea, Guam, the Philippines, Okinawa, and Korea and performed about eight shows a day right in the hospital wards, and then after the shows we would go bed to bed and shake hands with the GIs.

AW: And how did the GIs respond?

NS: Often times they would hand us a little note if they were from Colorado and they would say, "Please call my mom and dad and tell them that I'm alive, that I'm going to be OK, and let them know where I am." They asked us to send their love to their families. It was very moving. We saw a lot of horrific things in the wards of the hospitals.

The men and women who were injured in their beds would turn their mouths upward and express a smile. We would see feet tapping

NS: That was a very impactful moment. The young man in that photograph was thanking me for choosing to be in a war zone when he was not given a choice—he had to be in that war zone because of the draft. Our hearts just went out to these young men; they were only eighteen years old, in hand-to-hand combat in a war zone, and losing parts of their bodies and losing parts of their minds.

AW: You've mentioned to me that you watched a man receive a Purple Heart while you were performing next to him in his hospital bed. Can you tell me more about that experience?

NS: Yes, that was a very poignant moment, too. There were generals on both sides of his bed, and they asked our group to sing bedside upon giving him the Purple Heart. They pulled down the bed sheets to pin the heart on him, and that is when we learned he was a quadriplegic: he had no arms; he had no legs. I believe he stepped on a landmine or near a grenade to save some of his comrades, and he lost all of his limbs. It was devastating, it was shocking, it was very sad. I had very mixed emotions that this young man had sacrificed so much of himself for our freedom.

AW: How did that first tour impact your views on the war? What were your views before you left, and then when you came back?

NS: Well, that is a very large question. Prior to going into an active war zone we were college girls—young college girls—who, like

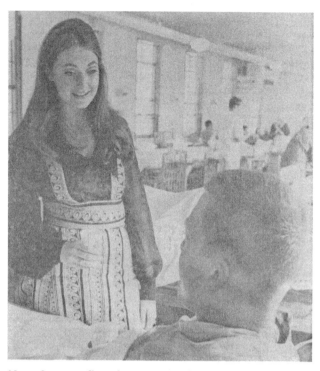

Nancy Stratton talks with a patient in a hospital ward during the USO Hardship Tour in the summer of 1970 (Rocky Mountain News)

through the sheets. And some people were clapping along with us; some were singing along with us. Just to see the wounded soldiers being inspired and happy in the moment—that we were taking their minds off of their pain and suffering—was wonderful. We were really an escape for them.

AW: There's a newspaper clipping of you standing next to one of the wounded soldiers in the hospital ward. What was going on in the photo?

most Americans, knew about a war going on, but we also were privy to the nightly newscasts of the Peace Movement. We knew that there was great division between the military efforts and the Peace Movement efforts in the United States. We were very honored to have been chosen to be a USO show, and we were caught up in the moment of that. As we went over there and started performing and sharing our music, and then upon living in a war zone right among the injured and active soldiers, we began to realize that this was real and that freedom had a very, very high price. We felt that the United States was the most phenomenal country in the world to live in because of the sacrifices generations of people have given in war efforts to maintain the freedom that we have in this country.

One thing that really stuck out when we returned from our first tour and got off the airplane at the San Francisco Airport was when we walked outside and there were big signs on the grass that said, "Dogs and GIs keep off the grass." That was a very poignant statement of where the World—the United States was called "the World" by the military overseas—was at during that time. GIs wanted to get back to the World but the World they were coming back to was very mixed as far as accepting what their mission was. So, we were conflicted when we came back. We empathized greatly with the military and their efforts because we saw firsthand what they had to do to maintain freedom in the United States.

AW: When did you go on your next USO tour?

NS: About two months after our return from the Hardship Tour, we received a letter from Mr. Sheldon stating that the USO Hollywood office had received hundreds of letters of

> "We were very honored and very excited about the chance to go back and share our music with more GIs."

gratitude and asked us to come back. We were granted a Christmas Special tour for thirty days during December of 1970. We were all still actively in school so we had to do the touring on our Christmas vacation. So, back we went, and this time we went only to Vietnam.

AW: How did you feel about all the great responses they received, and then to be invited back?

NS: We were thrilled. We were young women who were just going to college in Fort Collins and singing fun songs at rush parties and in different groups in Fort Collins, Colorado, and then all of a sudden we were performing for hundreds and thousands in the military. We were very honored and very excited about the chance to go back and share our music with more GIs.

AW: What was it like to return to Vietnam, stepping off the plane into a war zone again?

NS: Well the first word that comes to mind is "frightening." When the plane landed we were immediately whisked away through customs, with high security, and we were put into jeeps with armed security with us. We drove through the city of Saigon, and every political building was surrounded by coiled barbed wire and armed guards. We actually heard an explosion; we heard a loud pop sound and the jeeps immediately stopped. We girls thought that we were possibly being fired at, but it turned out that we had a blowout on the tire of one of the jeeps. That got the adrenaline flowing very quickly!

We stayed in buildings called BOQs (bachelor officer quarters), and they were very modestly appointed highrise hotel buildings in downtown Saigon. The windows were all taped with an "X," made out of four-inch-wide masking tape, so the glass would not shatter should we be under rocket attack in the city. I think, upon arriving at the BOQs, we truly realized we were in an active war zone and that we were in a very risky situation. We were morale builders; we had a positive effect on the troops so there was a price on our heads by the Viet Cong. Anything could happen at any moment.

One day we went back to our BOQ and were told that another BOQ two blocks away had been bombed by a Viet Cong who was disguised as a priest. That magnified the dangerous situation we were in, but it didn't matter. We were just high on the entire experience and the ability to bring an entertaining show to all the men and women that were over there.

AW: Tell me about your performances in Vietnam.

NS: For the majority of our thirty days in Vietnam, we would be flown out to remote firebases by helicopter. We would stand on a four-foot-high mound of dirt, and that was our stage. The GIs would just sit on the ground. We were performing on the edges of the jungles where most of the battle was taking place. And coming into a war zone, we always had machine gunners on either side of the helicopter doors in preparation for a possible attack as we landed.

We did a lot of cover songs from the Mamas & Papas and Peter, Paul, and Mary . . . that type of music, and we did a lot of original songs, in addition to Christmas songs. We had put together a one-hour show—and that was very difficult, to have enough songs to fill those sixty minutes. I remember our first encore that we received. We had no more songs left, so we just came back out and sang our opening song again, which was the "Colorado" song that we performed at every show. Funny and awkward things like that would happen along the way, but we pulled it off.

After every show we would go into the audience, and we would shake hands, give hugs, sign autographs. We received notes and letters to take back home to their families. We wanted to do that as much as possible.

AW: How did the GIs respond to having your group in Vietnam over the holidays?

Pictured right: Nancy Stratton

The Colorado Kappa Pickers performing aboard the USS Kitty Hawk

NS: I think it was special to them that we were there over the holidays, but it also made them homesick. On Christmas Eve, we played for a Marine camp that had been in the jungles for nine weeks. It was announced during the show that if some of the men didn't stop trying to get up on the stage, we would have to end the show. They just wanted to be close to us; we were singing Christmas songs, and I remember singing "Silent Night" and how somber everyone was—I saw tears on the faces of several men and women. The whole mood was very subdued, very spiritual, and a few people were overcome to the point where they *did* rush the stage (the mound of dirt), and we did have to stop the show. As the jeep was whisking us away, a GI ran up to me and handed me a belt. He said, "This is my treasure. I took this off of a Viet Cong this morning, and I want you to have it." We had several situations like that happen throughout the tour.

AW: Where else did you perform while in Vietnam?

NS: One of the most empowering and memorable experiences of our three tours we did was when we performed aboard the USS Kitty Hawk aircraft carrier in the demilitarized zone, which was between North and South Vietnam. We were five women on a ship that had three thousand sailors onboard. We spent three days there. In addition to our shows, we dined in the mess hall with the sailors and it was just very, very empowering. They had been at sea for about five months and had not seen people from back home—from the World—so needless to say our shows were very well received on the Kitty Hawk.

AW: You put yourself in so much danger on these tours. Why was it worth it to you?

NS: When you stand up and look out on the deck of a ship, for instance, at approximately five hundred people looking back at you, and what you are doing creates such joy and enthusiasm and happiness . . . it's an overwhelming rush of satisfaction. We truly brought a lot of laughter, a lot of music, a lot of happiness and joy to these men and women who were in the middle of a war, and it was just an incredible feeling to create that experience for them. That was our motivation; that was our purpose. Music was the vehicle that put us there, and we enjoyed lifting their spirits.

Scan to Listen

or visit
www.sombk.co/v1/95

"Colorado"
by The Colorado
Kappa Pickers

Music and lyrics by
David Allen and
Paul Colwell

*"Colorado" used with permission from
Nancy Stratton and Up with People*

"Music Isn't about Standing Still and Being Safe" —Miles Davis

by Bill Cushing

listen

two weeks after you died
a quarter-million thronged
by the St. Johns River
to hear the music you had spawned
hoping to see you
but
even in death
you never looked back

they were all there
    Hannibal   Bird
    Chick   Jo-Jo
    Red   Jaco
    Bean   Dizzy
    my favorite   Freddie Freeloader

isolated
you
    were a beacon
    a flagship for messages
        of the heart

back to the crowd   unbowed
that proud dance-walk
announced by muted horn
that spoke

and broke
through all the bull
and told us about a place

Miles

ahead of everyone else
you spent a lifetime
        thinking for yourself
        speaking to every generation
playing it all:
        jazz   blues
        funk   rock
        fusion
categories took
a backseat
to creativity
        and rhythm

                space

        and feeling
                spirit

I remember fourth grade
picking up a horn
then laying it down
rock and roll was my world
what did I know

seven years later I heard

it was in the Garden
where you brought me back
to music

I walked all the way home

Miles

from that train station
my head pounding with sounds
frantic-fast as the subway
I spent the night on
        those African rhythms
        you used decades
        before anyone else
        even thought to
filling my head
letting me know
I'd have it all down cold
if I could walk
as cool as the notes you heard
        coming from

Miles

you had that thing
        that style
that spark that was
a blue flame
        jumping
        off a gas stove
igniting everything   everywhere
touching the genetic
resonant
frequency
in all

Third Avenue & 85th Street, NYC

by Ruth Sabath Rosenthal

Waves of "Mood Indigo"
drew me to
a well-dressed crowd
ushered in a hush
bursting with flowers
leading to a stiff
in elegant tux
pleated shirt starched
as his expression

Duke Ellington
(yes in the flesh)

laid to rest
and I paid last respects
hastened home
on the cross-town bus
took the 'A' train
uptown
dug my 8-tracks up
and jived with the jazz man
into wee hours of night

A Wink from the Universe:
The improbable story of Surrender

by Ken Hamberg

In early 1987 three exceptionally talented and versatile musicians convened in a recording studio in Jamaica (Queens, the New York City borough, not the island) to begin recording what was then a standard three-song demo tape, meant to secure a contract with a major label record company. There were quite a few to choose from back then.

The studio, known as 1212, was located in a large rehearsal facility known as the Music Building, and it housed a motley collection of heavy metal bands (including Metallica and Anthrax), rap artists, soca and reggae bands, jazz and R&B musicians, and songwriters/producers, many of whom became 1212 clients.

Studio 1212 was originally founded and operated by the two musicians who played and wrote the songs on the demo. I was one of them. I performed the drums and keyboards, my partner and (still) best friend Mick contributed the guitars and basses, and Frank, vocalist *extraordinaire*, sang the songs, both leads and harmonies. We were entirely self-contained, including the production and the engineering.

That demo evolved into a full-length, elaborately produced independent recording that was roughly three years in the making. The time just flew; we were lost in the blur of blissful, creative myopia and the daily reality of trying to make a living as musicians. Eponymously titled *Surrender*, the name we'd decided upon for our project (and our band), the record sounded like a major sum of money had been spent on its fulfillment.

In fact the record was made on a shoestring budget, and a frayed one at that. It was recorded on studio down-time, late nights, and the occasional regular hours we booked with the odd record company development check. The "band" was never signed by any label, and by late 1990, when we finally sent out what had become a complete CD to more than 200 major record labels, radio stations, promoters, and producers, the gale-force winds of the grunge and alternative aesthetic had begun to blow in.

No one was interested in a glossy, cinematic-sounding record with wall-to-wall melodies and harmonies delivered by a singer blessed with an exquisite, bell-like tenor, performed with laser-like precision by musicians who could have been moonlighting from Journey or Yes.

The 80s were dead and buried. Another generation had arrived with its own look, sound, and perspective. Spandex and long 80s poodle-y curls had been replaced by plaid and long 90s unadorned braids. *Surrender* was almost comically irrelevant.

But it was also damn good. The record made us as much as we made the record. All of us believed we were creating a work of art. We hoped, like many other often-struggling musicians, that we would make some decent money from the record, so that we could record all the time and release our music more quickly to an adoring public. But I firmly believe that what really kept us interested and motivated was the fact that we were succeeding on an artistic and technical level that none of us had achieved before, on any project.

We thought we were creating a pop masterpiece, with *cojones.*

We couldn't conceive of the strange realities that lay ahead of us once we'd left the creative cocoon, because we were completely unequipped to handle the business part of making music.

We lived on our own planet, where "things happened" and we let things happen.

While we were recording *Surrender,* a cassette of a few of our songs made the rounds in Los Angeles and briefly wound up in rotation on several big rock radio stations. I have no idea how that happened, but we thought it was encouraging and didn't pursue it further.

After we began sending out the promotional CDs, we received several faxes

> "Nobody was interested in our record, and that was that. Enter the universe, and more specifically, the Internet."

from a Russian distributor requesting terms for a shipment of 30,000 copies. He thought we were an actual record company. We absolutely froze, having neither the funds nor the business acumen to address the situation. Years later a fan emailed me and told me that roughly 20,000 copies had been sold, that he knew of, in Russia alone; he'd bought his copy in the import section of a local record store. Apparently the distributor took matters into his own hands when he didn't hear back from us.

An A&R person from Epic Records got back to us immediately after he heard the CD and we began preparing for a label showcase in Los Angeles, fleshing out the band with some name-brand musicians willing to donate their time for rehearsal in exchange for a guaranteed spot on the inevitable tour. The A&R guy and his entire staff were fired several weeks into the proceedings, and we never heard from him again. Needless to say, there was no showcase.

An A&R guy from RCA's Urban Music division, who'd been a 1212 client, loved *Surrender* so much he wanted to put it out under his umbrella. That was apparently nixed; this wasn't "black music" and he was told to send it over to the Rock division (read "white music guys") who really understood material like *Surrender*'s. They passed, but encouraged us to re-submit once we'd updated our sound.

Absolutely nothing happened. No takers. The silence was deafening, and the apparent indifference on the part of the industry was crushing. Nobody was interested in our record, and that was that.

Enter the universe, and more specifically, the Internet.

In May 2003, a copy of the original promotional Surrender CD sold on eBay for $1,000. You can find one today on eBay available

"My mailbox was full for days with fans writing in from all over the world. It was absolutely surreal."

for $1,800. The most it has fetched that I know of is $2,500; the buyer, a nice Japanese fellow, contacted me via email and encouraged me to give the music a proper release. Apparently lots of people wanted the record but very few could afford it. He loved the music and thought that the band, not dealers and bootleggers, should be enjoying the proceeds.

The original Surrender CD, while musically successful, was a masterpiece in promotional ineptitude. The group members were not identified, nor were there any production credits as to who did what. The band photo was an easily lost insert, and the only contact information referred to a bogus production company housed in a

defunct recording studio (1212 burned down in 1995) with an out-of-service phone number. I have no idea what we were thinking, but if we wanted to enjoy anonymity we were very successful.

The results of the eBay sales apparently excited the curiosity and imagination of a number of Surrender fans from all over the world who decided to try to find out who and where we were. The most ambitious of these sleuth-fans congregated at a forum on a website called heavyharmonies.com, which is devoted to preserving rock as we no longer know it. They amassed pages and pages of informative and speculative chatter about Surrender.

They soldiered on. For three years. And we had no idea any of this was happening until March 2005.

I received a phone call at my home from a fan named Mike who was part of the team that had been tracking us down. He told me about the eBay sales. He knew the music very well, thought we were amazing, and wondered how we could have made such a record and then disappeared without a trace. Nobody knew anything about the band, but everybody cared. They cared about us, and our music . . . after 15 years. He just blew my mind.

Surrender had amassed a worldwide following of thousands who'd not only heard our music, but owned a copy. And we hadn't seen a dime, apart from a few leftover copies we'd sold on our own. I decided to go public, so with his help I posted an announcement on the forum, listed my email address, and said that if the response seemed to warrant it, I'd consider a proper release any fan could afford, as opposed to a coterie of wealthy collectors for whom a thousand dollars or more was chump change.

My mailbox was full for days with fans writing in from all over the world. It was absolutely surreal. I was in my own movie, moved to tears.

We released our Surrender album, calling it *Better Later Than Never* (a pun on the titles of the first and eighth tracks) in August 2005. Mick and I remastered it at his new studio in Manhattan, we hired a design firm to resurrect the original cover art and photo, and included a poster-quality insert that included the lyrics, liner notes, and yes, our names and proper credits. We hired a publicist to get the word out. We hired a web designer for our promotional website, surrendertunes.com. And we held the price of the CD to $12.00 (homage to Studio 1212).

It was a beautiful package, and the fans ate it up for months, at the rate of about 800 copies a week. It was a worldwide critical success as well, which was gratifying, and we went to Number 1 in Germany and the Benelux countries.

And it's still selling.

I'm never going to move a million records, or take a stroll on the moon, but I have a vault full of gold in my soul, and the fact that all of this happened, based solely on the music that we worked so hard to create, validates every minute we spent on it.

Listen to songs from Surrender's Better Later Than Never *(used with permission from Ken Hamberg). The full album is available for purchase at www.cdbaby.com/cd/surrendermusic.*

Scan to Listen
or visit
www.sombk.co/v1/103a

"Claire"
by Surrender

Scan to Listen
or visit
www.sombk.co/v1/103b

"Last Time I Say Goodbye"
by Surrender

Scan to Listen
or visit
www.sombk.co/v1/103c

"One Tough City"
by Surrender

High School

by Anna Alferova

This photograph captures a performance
by the band High School.

Vic Fuentes
by Jerin Micheal

Vic Fuentes of Pierce The Veil plays under a confetti shower at the O2 Academy Birmingham, England, on their sold out World Tour in 2015.

My Last Mix Tape

by Lynn L. Shattuck

After my brother's sudden death, there was just one thing I felt strong enough to do. Useless in the face of my parents' enormous grief and barely able to eat and sleep, I put together a mix tape for my brother's memorial service.

I spent hours hunched over my parents' stereo, which was tucked into a corner of their living room. From my perch, I could see the snow-stained Alaskan mountaintops through one of the large picture windows. One by one, I plucked songs for the tape then dubbed them, using the stereo's double cassette recorder as well as the newer, wired-in CD player. I couldn't focus enough to read a book or follow a sitcom, but my mind latched onto the job at hand. I obsessed over pressing the pause button at just the right second—you can't have too much silence on a mix tape, especially for a memorial service. The music helped loosen the clots of grief inside me.

My parents made the rest of the arrangements; they called the mortuary, placed the obituary, and reserved a space for the service. I leaned against the stereo, the vibration from the speaker rumbling against my spine.

***

In the shock-filled days after Will's death from heroin and alcohol, music was what first helped me cry.

It'd been two days since he'd died, and we went to a restaurant to try and eat.

A smiling waiter dropped off a basket of bread, and I picked around the edge of the crust. My brain ached from trying to comprehend the fact that Will, my only sibling, was dead. Pop songs blared in the background, stabbing against the words in my head: *Your brother is dead, your brother is dead.* The words looped through my mind, over and over again, nipping at the cottony buffer of shock that protected me from fully believing the truth.

I watched my parents peck at the bread, too, and I watched their eyes, swollen from crying. I'd almost cried the first morning after the news came, when I sat smoking cigarettes on the concrete stoop outside a friend's apartment. Crows circled overhead against the brightening sky. The city had slowly hummed to life as people woke up, drove to work or school. It seemed impossible that so much life was going on while my own had frozen.

Will won't get any more mornings, I'd thought. My chest clenched, sadness swelling up my throat.

I almost cried.

At the table, I stood up suddenly. "I need to get some air," I told my parents. "Do you want me to come with you?" my mom asked, already starting to stand. My dad looked up at me, concerned. I was a young adult, but my parents and I were clinging to each other as if I were a toddler.

"No, I just need a minute," I said. "I'm okay, really," I said, looking back at them.

I fled the restaurant, with its upside-down bicycles dangling from the ceiling and street signs hung at odd angles. I found a bench outside and sat. A nearby speaker brought the same music that played inside the restaurant, but away from the décor and people, it felt tolerable.

A new song started up, full of aching strings. The first lyrics slipped away from me, but I felt grateful for the slow tempo. On the road in front of me, cars stopped and went, stopped and went. Traffic lights hummed from red to green to yellow, then started over again. I exhaled for maybe the first time in days.

Then the chorus came; it was from "Helpless" by Neil Young.

The words expanded inside me, like one of those capsules you toss into a bowl of water and then watch as it becomes a big sponge dinosaur. They lifted off until there was just the sound of guitars, whining and winding, mimicking Young's voice. And there was something about the words and then the absence of them, and the sad, sad strings that made me hold my own knees like a baby. And finally, I cried.

***

Friends and family crowded my childhood home. When I needed space, I retreated to the front porch with my CD Walkman. Over and over again, I listened to Young's haunting "Helpless," which I'd bought the day after hearing it outside

"And now that he was gone, it was music that I turned to. Like him, it was untouchable, something I could feel but not see."

the restaurant. I was compelled to learn the words, to linger in them over and over again. People told me they were sorry for my loss, but their words felt hollow, their presence irritating. Instead it was the song, which wove itself around the cracked spot in my chest, that let me know I wasn't alone in my grief.

I sat on the porch, headphones pinned to my head, and sank into the music. Across from me was the rusting basketball hoop where my brother and I used to play Horse. I stared into the dark, wondering how my little brother, the co-keeper of my childhood, could be gone.

In many ways, we'd been opposites: Will was blue eyed, light haired, and pale skinned, while I was olive skinned with dark brown eyes and hair. He was outgoing and collected friends like baseball cards, and I was shy and clung to a few close buddies. He could be angry and rebellious, while I turned my emotions inwards and tended towards depression. But we shared a love of words, our mom's dark sense of humor, almond-shaped eyes, and a passion for music.

It was my little brother who first introduced me to Pearl Jam, and my little brother who had burst into my bedroom one April morning to tell me that Kurt Cobain

"Music was so central to who he was, to what he loved, and how he expressed himself."

had killed himself. He'd even followed in my footsteps by studying the music and video business program that I'd dropped out of a few years earlier. "I'm going to finish what Lynn started," he'd told our mom.

And now that he was gone, it was music that I turned to. Like him, it was untouchable, something I could feel but not see.

***

As I began making the mix tape for Will's memorial service, my mom handed me another cassette.

"You might want to use this," my mom said. "He made it for me last summer."

I listened to the entire tape, sobbing and singing along. There was one by Brad—a Seattle band I'd told my brother about—called "Some Never Make It Home." As the singer crooned about disappearing boys, I remembered hearing my brother's voice singing the song months earlier.

A few songs by Pedro the Lion—an indie-labeled Seattle band—were also on my mom's tape. I recognized them since Will had sent me the CD not long before he died. I'd felt a breeze of concern when I'd listened to the songs for the first time. The songs were spare and mournful, with lyrics hinting about needles and addiction, and they'd made me worry for my brother, who I knew had flirted with drugs.

Another song was one I'd never heard before: Starflyer 59's "Fell in Love at 22." I played it, then instantly hit rewind, trying to catch the words. The song was so short, the lilting music so bittersweet; each time I listened to it, I mourned how quickly it was over. Even the title of the song hit home—my brother was twenty-one when he died, and would stay that age. Twenty-two was unreachable.

The tape he'd made for our mom was so *Will*—how many twenty-one-year-olds make mix tapes for their mothers? While he could be difficult and angry, music provided him with a way to reveal his sensitivity.

As I collected the songs for the tape, some from Will's extensive CD collection, others from my parents' cassettes, and a handful of my own favorites, I worried it wouldn't be good enough, and that Will wouldn't approve. Music was so central to who he was, to what he loved, and how he expressed himself. Music twinned us, giving us something in common that we hadn't inherited from either of our parents.

On the day of his service, I pulled on a black knee-length dress and my great-aunt's silver-grey cardigan. I grasped the plastic cassette

110

case in my palm. "I don't want to go," I told my parents. To go to the memorial service, to face all those people who'd quickly assimilated his death, would make Will's death real, permanent.

"I know, baby," my mom said, wiping her dark eyes. My dad looked pale in his dark suit, his eyes downcast.

"Do we have to?" I asked. I felt like a little girl who wanted to stay home from school, not a twenty-four-year-old woman. My parents nodded.

My parents had reserved a wood-floored ballroom near the water for the service. The room was familiar—we'd gone to Christmas parties and attended plays there. I couldn't believe we were there to mark my brother's death.

Friends and family shuffled in. After a handful of people told stories about Will, I started the tape. People milled about the room, leaving memories of my brother in the guest book or catching up with old friends. "Helpless" came on first and I saw a hollowed look sweep across my brother's best friend's face.

A mellow Elton John song, "Curtains," with haunting, poetic lyrics, was next. Our dad was a huge Elton John fan growing up. He was a family favorite, and I remembered many times in the car when we'd all sing along to "I Guess That's Why They Call It the Blues," or the more somber John Lennon tribute, "Empty Garden."

People lined up to hug us. "Be strong for your parents," several people implored me. A friend of my parents hugged me and suggested I see a grief counselor. I felt like I was suffocating from all the people and words and unrequested advice.

The music was too quiet. I imagined my brother making fun of me for picking so many mellow songs. I had a quick image of him

"We sat there in silence, the songs swirling around us, eerie and heartbreaking."

slamming out a punk version of "Leaving on a Jet Plane" on my electric guitar, his face wild, while his friends and I laughed.

I walked away from the receiving line and cranked the volume on the music. A few older guests glanced towards me, jarred by the volume. I didn't care. I was tired of standing there, listening to people ask me to take care of my parents. Didn't they realize how much I was hurting, too? Besides, Will would love that I was blasting music for him.

When a Pedro the Lion song came on, another friend of my brother, who was battling a drug addiction of his own, looked overcome. I sunk down next to him on the edge of the stage and reached my arm around his back. Though it was a warm day, he wore a leather jacket. I guessed that the jacket was to hide needle marks freckling his arms.

We sat there in silence, the songs swirling around us, eerie and heartbreaking. We sat through Pearl Jam's "Release," Eddie Vedder's mantra-like ode to his departed dad. My eyes filled up when Starflyer 59's too fast "Fell in Love at 22" floated through. I could feel people watching me, wondering and worrying. Every few minutes I'd scan the room for my parents to make sure they were still standing.

And then the tape was over, and the service was over.

My parents and I returned home to a living room full of flowers and the beginning of the end of our shock. The formalities had played out—the service had been attended, the obituary printed. All that was left was to step into our blinding, tuneless grief.

***

Will's CD collection rests in my basement office, one of the few things of his I can't bear to part with, even sixteen years after his death. I wonder what music my brother would be into now if he were still alive—if he'd have new favorites or if that old Seattle music would still quicken his pulse and make him tap his feet. I think of how much he'd love the technology we've acquired: the ability to tap a screen and have a song drop down into our cell phones or iPods, as if by magic. I imagine him blowing entire paychecks on songs, obsessively rearranging playlists with the swipe of a finger.

But with the ease of downloadable music, which can be acquired on a whim, it's different. Sitting in the living room of my childhood home, hitting pause and record over and over again, watching the CDs spin and the shiny tape wind around itself, was part of a process. While I tried to capture my brother in the songs I picked, I was instead creating a soundtrack for my loss. Those songs—the choosing and the surrendering to them—helped ensure that I didn't turn away from my pain. Grief is analog, after all. It is bumpy and imperfect, full of awkward pauses and tangled brown tape. There is nothing smooth, instant, or easy about it. You have to sit through it like I did. You have to endure.

Old Lovers

by Jamie Virostko

A tired café on a nameless eve,
Fluorescents and grinders severed the night.
Single-minded patrons clacked on laptops.
Unaware of their brethren,
All spirits lost to the infinite net.

A gangly tattered man drifted silently in.
Uneven silver tresses obscured his somber visage.
Gazing downward, he slung a black, battered case.
To an empty corner, he settled unnoticed;
And from that old box, his eternal lady was unbound.

Custom forged, she lounged in the bend of his knee.
Graffiti-scratched filigree nestled her arcs.
The ancient tree of her birth
Infused in her essence, the fecund soil
And smoldering amber of fading dusk.

A single stroke—she trembled awake.
Curious heads popped above brain-numbing screens.
In suspended vibration,
Timbered curves he caressed.
Drawing a breath, a seduction began.

Long rigid fingernails fomented her strings.
Nimble callouses rippled in rapids traversing her neck.
Frenzied kisses lavished startling strums.
Resonant waves tore through the air
Like microscopic gnomes run amok.

Dawn rising over an earth-shuddering beat;
Shards of hope spun as stardust:
Visceral, pounding, and primal,
Overwhelming delicacy burst in a flash of funk,
Laying souls bare as natural as love.

Evanescent bullion trickled beyond boundaries
Where the past is unfettered and the future rang pure.
His countenance thrust aft, the tousled curtain parted.
Vigorous serenity brought all to surrender
And light to the sorrow of bloodshot eyes.

A pressed, quelling palm and he silenced his wife.
More than sweet sound, her gift gave true life.

Music Colors
My Life

by Alland Dharmawan

Taken at Bromo, Indonesia, this photo depicts the harmony of music and nature. The beautiful sound of cello dances with the breeze.

Grace

by Bar Scott

I was twenty-eight when I bought a small house next to West Laurel Hill Cemetery outside of Philadelphia. It was 1986. My grandparents had been buried there a couple of years earlier, so I would often walk to their spot and say hello. Their son, William was buried there, too. He died when he was two from complications of spina bifida. There's only one stone for the three of them. Will's name is carved on the side. You wouldn't see it unless you knew to look. I like that they're all there together. It tells me something about the longevity of love. My mother was born shortly before Will died, so she only remembers the absence of him.

While I was living in that house I bought a small Casio keyboard to see if I could sing and play at the same time. It was small enough that I could carry it around, so one summer afternoon I took it up to my bedroom and lay down with it on my belly. I cycled through the sounds it could make to see if any of them would inspire me to sing along. I was just starting to write songs back then. Like most keyboards, my Casio had a synthesized vocal patch that sounded like a hundred voices singing in unison. With the push of a key a choir would sing "Ah" for as many seconds as you were willing to hold it down. A low D-flat sounded good to me that afternoon, so I held it and started to sing.

When I was in high school I sang in the school and church choirs. Those were medium-sized (25 to 30 people). In my senior year I was invited to audition for the Pennsylvania State Choir. I say "State," but I don't actually remember if it was State, County, or Regional. All I know is that it was big, and we were good. There were 200 of us. I was an alto. With all those voices singing together we could produce a lot of sound. What was more amazing, though, was that we could create a profound silence, too. We sang so quietly at times that I could feel my body lift away from my feet. During one of our concerts, I sang a solo on a spiritual called "Deep River." As 199 singers hummed quietly behind me, I stepped forward and sang as earnestly as I knew how.

There are moments in my past that I'm sure have brought me to where I am now. That solo was one of them. Standing in front of an audience with a choir of singers behind me was both exhilarating and humbling. The sound of sustained human voices in harmony is one that has always moved me, but that night was the first time I was aware of it.

So when I turned my Casio on and played a D-flat for what must have been twenty minutes, it was natural for me to sing something that sounded like a hymn. "Grace" is the song and melody that came out of that bedroom experiment. The song is a chant with a Celtic feel. It has only one line of lyrics: "Thank the world for

> "As 199 singers hummed quietly behind me, I stepped forward and sang as earnestly as I knew how."

giving me all the reasons that I have to sing." The rest of the melody is vocalized on various vowel sounds depending on my mood when I sing it.

The first time I sang "Grace" for anyone else was for my extended family. I asked my father in advance if I could say grace at our upcoming Thanksgiving dinner. Saying grace had always been his job, but he was glad to have me do it. Looking back, asking for this change in routine was a testament to my need to be heard.

When I started to sing my grace, forty-five family members sitting at uneven tables pushed together stared back at me. I was scared. There was so much to lose. If they didn't like my song, or if they were uncomfortable with the time it took me to sing it, or if I would sing out of tune or lose my place, they'd cast me out. Reject me forever. But they didn't. When I started to sing, they got quiet and lowered their heads.

I've sung "Grace" in some remarkable places since that night. On New Year's Eve in 2005, I sang it in the Cathedral Church of St. John the Divine in New York City—the largest gothic cathedral in North America. The place was packed with over 3,000 people. The spotlights were bright, and the space was so big that I couldn't see faces beyond the first row. There was no reason to be afraid; the lyrics were easy to remember and the melody was mine to improvise. I was more excited than scared.

I stood in the center of the sacristy as the organist began to play a low D-flat on the pipe organ behind me. I'd learned during my soundcheck that whatever I sang would linger in the room for a long time—"eight seconds," the sound engineer told me. Because of that, I sang my lines slowly and waited for each phrase to disappear before I sang the next one. Controlling the time like that was thrilling: the silence between phrases, the harmonics that lingered and bounced off the masonry walls. It was as beautiful a sound as I'd ever heard. It was hard to believe it was coming from me. Yet somehow I knew there was more to it than that.

In late February 2002 I got a call from a filmmaker named Rick who had heard me sing at a concert in Upper Black Eddy, Pennsylvania, a few years earlier. After he introduced himself, he said, "I'm doing a film on the healing power of music. I'd like you to be a part of it." As he described his project my eyes filled up with tears, and my heart felt bigger in my chest. I felt as though I were being rescued. My son Forrest had died two weeks earlier. He was three-and-a-half. He'd been diagnosed with liver cancer when he was two. I was still in shock. Rick's call reminded me that I would be ok.

Two months later when his film was finished, Rick introduced me to a woman who lost her husband on 9/11. She was planning a concert at the Beacon Theatre in New York City to thank the 2,500 first-responders who tried to find her husband in the rubble. Phoebe Snow, Beth Nielsen Chapman, Delores Holmes, and I were asked to headline the event.

A week before the concert, we were invited to Ground Zero. Escort vehicles and Port Authority personnel, who worked in the pit for months, met us at the upper gates. The cleanup had finally ended. It was July. The sun was bright and beginning to set. We climbed into police vehicles and drove into the deep, gray-white earth. The trip was slow and reverent. So many lives had been lost there. At the bottom, one of the policemen told us to wander around to get a feel for the place. He wanted us to understand what they felt like down there.

We took off one by one. It was a time for solitude and reflection. The ground was uneven and hard. I was aware that I was walking on bedrock. The sixty-five-foot concrete walls that had supported the towers were sheer and covered with rusty cuts and scrapes. The subway tunnels looked like giant conduits that could empty into the vast concrete pool we were standing in. I felt like I'd drown if someone turned the water on. Stairwells led nowhere. A fine, moist dust from pulverized computers, phones, light fixtures, and everything else that died there covered everything. It was silent despite the busy streets above us.

When our group gathered again forty-five minutes later, Rick asked, "Do you think you could sing "Grace" for us?" I dropped my eyes to the ground and said yes.

After a moment I took a shallow breath and started to hum. I looked over at Dolores

"When I started to sing, they got quiet and lowered their heads."

and her sisters and encouraged them to join me. Once they were humming I took another breath and started the melody. I thought of Forrest and smiled. I looked around at everyone there, then looked up at the sky. I thought about the day the towers fell and all that had happened since then, and I could feel my tears. Yet there I was singing, my body filled with joy and sorrow. How had all of this happened? How could it be that I was singing in this incredible place? Or that my song created with a Casio keyboard on a summer afternoon would be a comfort to people who experienced such loss?

When the concert started the following week, the lights went down and the show began with a short film. The opening scene was of me singing "Grace" in the pit. I hadn't realized I was being filmed. What I noticed as I watched was that the Port Authority policemen who had taken us down there were crying while I sang. These were men who would not have cried before 9/11. I call that grace.

Scan to Listen
or visit
www.sombk.co/v1/121

"Grace"
by Bar Scott

"Grace" used with permission from Bar Scott

121

Music Making 2

by Vinesh Rajpaul

This is the towering and sonically incredible Dobson Opus 91 organ in Merton College's Chapel in Oxford, England.

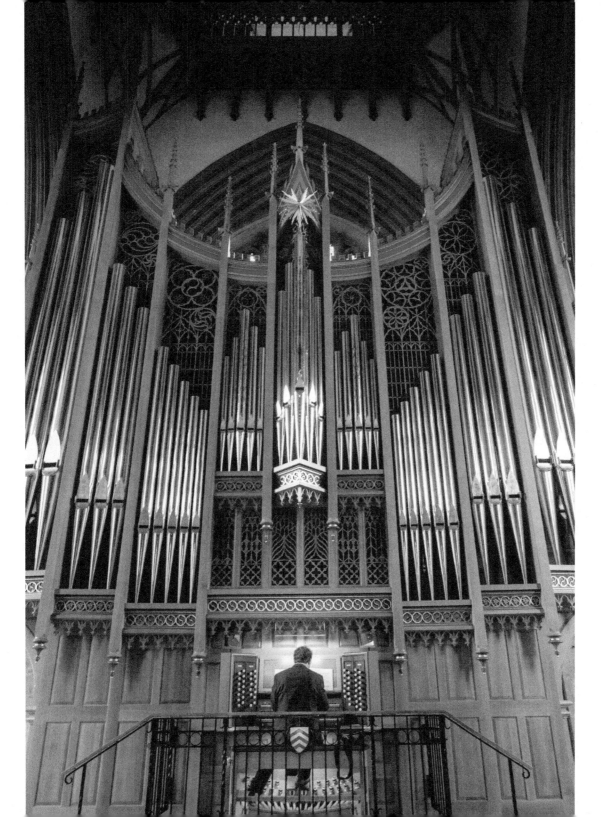

A Bluesman in Bosnia

by Amanda Schreier

At the height of the Bosnian War in a city under siege, Mili Tiro left the charred sanctuary of his apartment home in Mostar, guitar in hand, and walked to the front line to play the blues.

That was over twenty years ago. Today, Tiro is the executive producer of the Mostar Blues & Rock Festival, now celebrating its thirteenth year. Although Bosnia may seem like a strange place for the blues to take root, Tiro has used his passion for the music of the American South as a way to help heal his divided city after war tore it apart.

Tucked away on the banks of the aqua-blue Neretva River, Mostar is a quaint mountain town in Bosnia, best known for its Ottoman architecture and the ancient, hand-carved stone bridge that has spanned the river since the sixteenth century. The old bridge, or "Stari Most," is where the city got its name: Mostar literally means "bridge-keeper" in Bosnian.

I first met Tiro in the summer of 2004, almost ten years after the end of the Bosnian war. I was in Mostar researching the use of music in helping to reestablish trust and bridge ethnic divisions after the war. The European Union, US State Department, and several international aid organizations had tapped into Mostar's rich legacy of multiculturalism and the arts to try and encourage peace-building through music, with modest success. Several officials mentioned the work of a local music center dedicated to helping victims of war overcome their trauma, of which Tiro was the program coordinator.

One of the first things Tiro showed me upon meeting was his collection of records—some old rhythm and blues—an anthology of tattered vinyl memories from his youth. The albums survived the war, a remarkable feat of which Tiro was clearly proud.

When Tiro speaks, he has a steady, soothing voice, but he reveals little emotion except for when he talks about music. Now in his late forties, he has the weathered look of a man who has lived too much history in too short of a time. But his wavy, chin-length black hair hints at a rock 'n' roll youth; his lifelong passion has helped keep him grounded from the horrors of war and its persistent aftermath.

Having grown up in Bosnia and survived the war, Tiro seems to identify more with being a musician than he does with any ethnic or religious affiliation. He has never told me which ethnic group he belongs to—Bosniak, Croat, Serb— probably because it was the exaggeration of the divisions that led to four years of war and continues to poison the political climate of the country today.

Mili Tiro (photo courtesy of Mili Tiro and the Mostar Blues & Rock Festival)

While ethnicity and religion are still often used in Bosnia as a tool to encourage the differences between people, music—especially the blues—taps into the common experience of being human.

"It is the music of truth," Tiro explained. "In it, I hear the stories of ordinary men, of everyday things: pain, happiness, survival, love, and pride. It struck me that when it comes to the blues you cannot like it just a little or fake it. There is nothing commercial about it. Blues is like religion—you either get the call or you don't."

For Tiro, that call came in the early 1980s when he got his first blues album. "Records, especially rock and blues, weren't all that easy to get a hold of in Yugoslavia," he recalled. "Yet, we somehow managed, mostly thanks to friends who traveled abroad. I was listening to rock music,

"Tiro never stopped playing music during the war."

but when a friend gave me the albums of Muddy Waters and John Lee Hooker, I was hooked."

In high school, Tiro and his friends got summer jobs and used the money to buy their first instruments. "We started making noise in the basement, having fights with neighbors. It was great. It was the best part of my life."

He paused. "And then what happened, happened."

In 1993, Mostar was destroyed during the Yugoslav wars, the worst violence in Europe since the Holocaust. Mostar was once known as a bastion of culture and diversity in the former Yugoslavia. But the ethnic war between the Orthodox Serbs, Catholic Croats, and Muslim Bosniaks turned neighbors into enemies and transformed the city into a battleground. Mostar was eventually divided into two distinct ethnic enclaves: the Croatian militia laid siege to the Bosniak population, trapping them for nine months on the isolated, eastern side of the river.

Tiro never stopped playing music during the war.

The frontline, known as the Boulevard, was the dividing line between the two warring sides. When it wasn't too dangerous, Tiro would grab his guitar and meet his friends there to play music.

"Often, we could sense a similar atmosphere on the other side of the battlefield. We could hear the same songs," he said.

Tiro was part of a generation that played music, painted, and acted in theaters, but then the war came and threatened to take away everything and everyone he cared about.

"Many of my friends left for other countries, many died. This generation of mine just perished." Tiro used music as a way to rebel against what was happening to him and the city he loved.

"That guitar survived," he said. "First guitar I bought. I also managed to save a lot of my vinyl records. Lots of them. I used to take them out when my flat was on fire."

He smiled. "So, as you can tell, I can't live without music."

By the time the war ended in Bosnia in 1995, Mostar was divided and lay in ruin. Even the famous old bridge, which had survived both World Wars, was destroyed in the conflict. The destruction of Mostar's bridges came to symbolize the difficulty in reuniting what was now a mentally and physically divided city—with Bosniaks living in the east and Croats in the west. That's when music began to play a significant role in the reconciliation and recovery of Mostar.

In 1997, the Italian tenor Luciano Pavarotti opened a music center on the eastern banks of the Neretva River in an old school building that survived the war. Tiro became the program coordinator. It was his job to organize events like artist-themed workshops, poetry readings, dance performances, theater shows, and of course, concerts. The center also had a recording studio—the best in the former Yugoslavia, according to Tiro—and the first ever music therapy program in the Balkans. Pavarotti wanted to use the arts to foster a safe, engaging environment where all people in Mostar could feel welcome.

Once the Pavarotti Music Center was complete and the bridges were rebuilt, the musicians needed a way to get people to actually cross the bridges and come to the center. The solution: two international vans.

"We could cross the ethnic lines and go through the city because of the international plates," Tiro explained. In the early years after the war, the city was governed by the European Union, and the international plates allowed people to travel throughout the city without identifying their ethnic affiliation. "We would bring people from the west side here to play music."

In 2003, Tiro and a group of like-minded musicians founded the Mostar Blues & Rock Festival to coincide with America's celebration of one hundred years of the blues. It was held at the Pavarotti Music Center. The festival's co-producers Orhan "Oha" Maslo and Stephen Long explained that, after the war, cultural expression in Mostar stagnated.

"In those times," Long said, "Mostar was a silent city, like a ghost town." Few events were held and the town was still very much divided, both physically and mentally. "The consequences of the war are still felt today, but in 2003 it was fresh."

Stari Most Bridge in Mostar, Bosnia

Maslo recalled that maybe one hundred people showed up for that first concert, but since then, the festival's popularity has grown, and it now attracts several thousand participants every year. Still, funding continues to be an issue.

"If there was no international support, we would not be able to survive at all," Maslo admitted.

The festival receives the majority of its funding from donors and sponsors like the US State Department, the City of Mostar, and the Bosnian Cultural Ministry, as well as revenues from ticket sales. According to Tiro, the festival has become an important event for Mostar, particularly when it comes to tourism, because it attracts visitors from the entire region, helping to improve the image of the city and Bosnia as a whole.

Since its inception, the Mostar Blues & Rock Festival has attracted a number of local and international blues and rock artists, of which Tiro is proud. "It does feel good to say that Snowy White, Danny Shepard, Tito & Tarantula, Big Brother & The Holding Company, Ana Popovic, and many others have performed in Mostar."

The 13th Annual Mostar Blues & Rock Festival was held from July 16 to 18, 2015, and Tiro was excited they were able to arrange yet another great lineup: Mike Zito & The Wheel, Nine Below Zero, Big Dez, Delta Blues Gang, Night Train Blues Band, Jolly Jumper & Big Moe, and the Rock School Blues Band. "We also introduced some young blues and rock performers, which has always been one of the goals of the festival," he said.

Nevertheless, despite the renewed cultural expression, the concerts, and the reconstruction of the old bridge, the struggles still facing Mostar are vast. Many public services—such as post offices, electric companies, bus stations, and emergency response—run complicated parallel institutions absurdly divided along ethnic lines that threaten to bankrupt an already struggling economy. Last year, rioters took to the streets in Bosnia's biggest cities, including Mostar, and set fire to government buildings in protest over corruption, high unemployment, and the deteriorating political climate. Bosnia also experienced the worst flooding in living memory, leaving behind several billion dollars of catastrophic destruction, quite possibly worse than the physical damage caused during the 1992-1995 war.

Still, Tiro remains hopeful. "Mostar is healing," he said, "slowly rising from the dust. We must educate the generations to come to foster tolerance. We are already heading in that direction, but there's still a lot of work to be done."

Tiro lowered his voice and sighed deeply. "After the war, I saw in the newspapers they called Mostar the European Hiroshima, so you can imagine how it looked."

Even today the remnants of war are all too close. The stone buildings that line the Boulevard are potted with bullet holes and missing chucks, reminders of the up-close, personal combat that engulfed this region only twenty years ago.

"Today it is not something good, but it is much better than it was," Tiro said as a gentle smile spread across his somber face. "Now there are concerts instead of war."

For more information on the Mostar Blues & Rock Festival, visit www.MostarBlues.com.

Mili Tiro at the Mostar Blues & Rock Festival
(photo courtesy of Mili Tiro and the Mostar Blues & Rock Festival)

45

by Evelyn Hampton

Once I dreamt I had all the records ever made,
45s filling my bedroom top to bottom.
I woke up deliriously happy, only
to find it was just a dream.
   Just a dream, just a dream . . .

My brother drilled me every day:
name the B-side, label, singer, songwriter.
He would whistle the tune; I'd better get it right
the same way I'd have to know
the make and model of every car on the road.

Never stacked our records
like the other kids did.
They were stored in their paper jackets,
lined up on a shelf like little soldiers
and tabbed with an alphabetical marker.

Decca, RCA, Chess, Sun, Atlantic, Motown.
We rocked, we rolled, we twisted, we strolled.
They spun on the old phonograph
that my brother carried home on his bike
from the Green Stamp store.

Those vinyl treasures accumulated
and the years passed.
We packed them and moved them
from place to place until eventually
they were hidden away in some cabinet.

Technology had moved on.
They were "oldies" now.
Music had moved on.
We were "oldies" now.

Someday, my grandchildren
will be cleaning out our belongings
and come across these strange black vinyl disks.
They'll have a good laugh and shake their heads.
Decca, RCA, Chess, Sun, Atlantic, Motown: trash.

Requiem

by Aaron Parrett

The breathing tube lying like a tentacle across my uncle's face pulsed with a harsh rhythm, the machine noise reminding the few of us gathered in the room that his time was growing short. The steady drip of morphine kept him on the brink of sleep, and his skin was sallow. Still, he managed to open one eye, feebly, and lift his fingers in the semblance of a wave the moment he heard me draw my bow across the strings of my fiddle.

A nurse with a kind face and soft voice had told us a few hours before that the surgeons had decided not to operate. He was too weak to make it through another traumatic procedure. It was time to think about what his wishes might be for the last stage of life, she said.

"We'll make him comfortable and make sure he isn't in any pain," she quietly reassured us.

I could tell by the faint lines of sadness at the corners of her eyes that she was used to bearing such unwelcome messages to weary families. Even if a person has, through the years, learned to finesse an announcement of death, it's all but impossible to return to work undiminished from such a mission.

"We have a harpist who, if you'd like, will come in and play," she added. "Some folks find the music soothing for the transition."

I admired her, this woman who sought to soften sorrow with song.

My uncle Bud had grown up during the Great Depression, with parents who cared more about beer and cigarettes than food and schooling. When he was ten years old, he paid for piano lessons from money he earned himself washing ore for placer miners farther up the gulch where they lived in western Montana. My uncle walked each Sunday afternoon a couple of miles to the teacher's house, where she coached him through a John Thompson beginner's book. All week long he would practice on an old piano his folks had relegated to the woodshed, as it took up too much room in their small cabin. Even in winter, when it was cold enough to see his breath and he had to wear gloves, he would force himself to go out to the shed and run through his scales and chords and inversions.

"I was desperate to be a musician," he once said. "But after a few years, I realized that I'd gotten about as good as I would ever get, and that was all right."

Instead, he became a carpenter and built a string of houses, one after the other, all by himself. He'd buy a lot somewhere and put up a shed or garage, and then a house, performing every phase of construction himself, from pouring the foundation to nailing the shingles on the roof. He would furnish them and live in each one for a while, until he got bored and started looking around for a new lot. And in every single house he built, he put a piano in the living room.

He was forty years old when I was born—I was the first child of his younger brother—and I grew up his inevitable apprentice. My uncle taught me to run a saw, the correct way to hold a hammer, and the difference between a rafter and a purlin. In the evenings, after dinner, he'd invariably put a hefty pinch of Copenhagen in his lip and sit down at the piano. He liked to play the songs that were popular when his own parents were young: "Sidewalks of New York," "My Gal Sal," "Meet Me in St. Louis," "In the Shade of the Old Apple Tree," and many others tunes, the names of which I've forgotten. When I was in high school, he encouraged me to get a guitar and learn a few chords so we could play together.

It sounds odd to say this now, but I came from a family that was not musical. My sister took piano lessons as a kid, but her heart wasn't in it, and neither of my parents could carry a tune. It's true, my uncle played, and I did get a guitar and learned enough chords to strum along with his piano playing, but I could see that the ratio of practice to accomplishment was too far out of whack to suggest even a hint of talent or promise.

It didn't take me long to get about as good as I would ever get, but—as my uncle put it—that was all right.

Along the way, I learned just what led my uncle to forsake his dream of becoming a concert pianist: it was impossible, among other things, for him to play any song that was not a waltz. And if the song was not a waltz, he played it in waltz rhythm anyway. When I pointed out once that "Am I Blue," for example, was supposed to be cut time, and that I was finding it impossible to accompany him, he seemed surprised.

"Don't you like waltzes?" he asked.

"Well, sure," I said. "But that song's not a waltz."

He shrugged. "Well," he said. "I guess I just like that rhythm."

"He then said something to me that changed the way I thought about myself and music and my family. . . ."

In graduate school I traded my guitar for an old violin and learned a few old-time fiddle tunes. Meanwhile, my father, now in his fifties, got himself a guitar and started taking lessons.

"I'm afraid I started a bit late," my father once confessed to his teacher.

"What do you mean, late?" the teacher replied. "You've got until you die."

This is what I mean when I say we were not a musical family.

I think my uncle was proud that I persisted and that eventually I even played in a few bands, performing on occasion in local bars. My uncle would come out to see us when he could, enthusiastically stamping his foot, and clapping after every number.

I cringed once when I heard him bragging about me to one of his neighbors sitting at the bar. Afterward I told my uncle that I wasn't really much of a musician, and I phrased it in a way that implied he wasn't either. He looked at me for a while with eyes that had seen a lot of things during the Depression. He then said something to me that changed the way I thought about myself and music and my family:

"It's mainly about whether you enjoy it or not," he said. "I don't know about you," he went on, "but I've gotten a hell of a lot of satisfaction out of music over the years."

That was why, many years later when we gathered around his death bed, my ears perked up when the nurse mentioned a harpist.

I asked her if I could go out to my truck and get my fiddle.

"Of course," she said.

The last sign my uncle gave that he was still in this world was a frail wave of his hand that bade me to play. And so, amid the blinking machines and the antiseptic odor of his hospital room, I played the tunes he loved as best I could: "Red River Valley," "Amazing Grace," and "Train on the Island." When they disconnected the tubes and his breathing became ragged and arrhythmic, I played because I knew that he could hear it somehow, still, and that my amateur sawing was as pleasing to him as the prospect of one more day on earth.

Amateur as we were, we shared music the way other people pass heirlooms along from generation to generation. Even though no antique dealer would hazard a passing glance at most of the objects families tend to cling to and value, some of those things become symbols of continuity, of an ineffable history that ensures some semblance of what has gone before will endure for those we leave behind.

"Playing music is difficult," my uncle once told me. "Hell," he said, "if it were easy, everyone would do it." Somehow, the expertise that eluded us connected us across generations the way an old bureau or a grandfather clock might have.

In the end, my uncle passed from this world into the next with the rough and scratchy sound of my fiddle to guide him, and I don't think he would have wanted it any other way.

The Voice of Those That Weep

by Richard LeBlond

It happened while I was doing the dishes.

It happened because of an odd thing that has come with aging, in a long parade of odd things. The music I listen to has gotten older. Music is important in my life, as it is for most people. In recent years I have become increasingly attracted to music of the Renaissance. In my neck of the world, its fan base is incredibly small. Many of my friends regard it as a harmless but unlistenable personality defect.

Almost all of the music I am passionate about—from the late 1400s to early 1600s—comes from a time of fatalism and poverty, of plague and the Inquisition, of common childhood mortality, of dangerous medicine. Aging opened me up to what I think is the purpose of this music: it's a drug for the soul, always ethereal, occasionally ecstatic. The polyphony beckons full engagement. And sometimes the music becomes personal, digging deep into my psyche and soul.

It happened as I listened to the motet, "*Versa est in luctum*," from a mass for the dead composed by a Spanish priest during the Inquisition. His name is Tomás Luis de Victoria, and he composed some of the most emotionally powerful music I have heard. I had no idea music like this was being written long before Mahler and the Righteous Brothers.

The motet has a hook in it, a slowly pulsating wail about halfway through the four-minute work. As it floats above the mourners, the wail is intensified by its restraint.

It happened even though I had heard the piece a dozen times. As I stood there washing the dishes, the wail came, and I fell to the floor sobbing nearly to suffocation, my body heaving. I had been overcome by the strongest feeling of grief I have ever experienced. I was grieving for everyone I have ever loved who is gone. It was the first time I had openly, passionately grieved for my mother, whose death affected me the most. I grieved for many friends—too many—among the departed. And I grieved for my father, which was a long time coming.

"*Versa est in luctum cithara mea . . . My harp is turned to mourning*, and my music into the voice of those that weep."

It has become a reminder to love more those who remain.

The author was listening to "Versa est in luctum" by Tomas Luis de Victoria performed by Gabrieli Consort with William Lyons under the direction of Paul McCreesh

'Til My Twilight Years

by Carlo Zamora

This is my interpretation of classical music that has been loved until the twilight years of people of music.

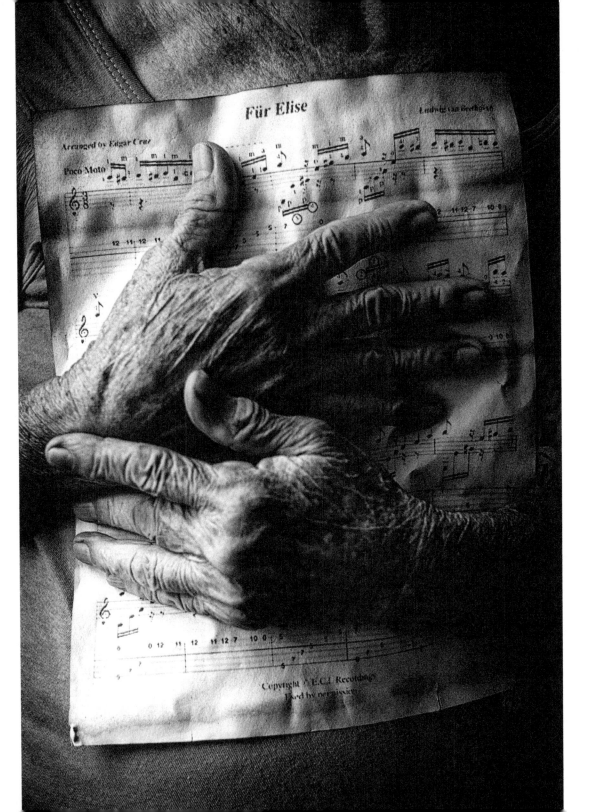

What but the Music

by Kenneth Salzmann

Maybe graying women and balding men are gathering
right now in every improbable town that hugs
a two-digit highway pointing vaguely toward America.

Maybe it's turning out we are unremarkable, after all—
unique and universal, just like all the rest.

Maybe it's nothing but the same comfortable crawl
every generation makes toward first things and well-worn
memories, when they start to notice the obituaries
are piling up higher than anyone ever thought they could.

Or maybe it *is* the music, after all.

What but the music might have orchestrated
forgotten revolutions and unforgettable kisses?
What but the music underscored every presumed
triumph and defeat, drew us into church basements
and into cheap apartments in bad neighborhoods,
ripped down walls, egged us on, played us out?

(Some of us never thought we'd make it this far,
and some of us were right.)

But maybe a soundtrack laid down decades ago
can permeate our souls and chart our lives
until one day we begin to see—long after we've
stopped looking—that astonishing rhythms
really did change the world.

What but the music might have bound us then?
What but the music might bind us again?

Cuban Musicians
by David Roberts

This scene was taken in Santiago de Cuba and captures a lovely impromptu performance by these old time musicians.

About Hungry for Music

Hungry for Music is a non-profit organization that supports music education and cultural enrichment by acquiring and distributing quality musical instruments to underserved children with willing instructors and a hunger to play. At Hungry for Music, their most important service is putting musical instruments into hungry hands. They serve children who demonstrate a desire to learn music as well as teachers who have students willing to learn.

By sharing instruments and musical experiences, Hungry for Music gives children, who would not normally have the opportunity, to experience a kind of freedom and self-discovery that is often stifled in an atmosphere of economic hardship. All of their events, benefits, instrument drives, and CD production are aimed at uplifting those lives and enriching culture at large by spreading the availability of music education.

Hungry for Music, founded by Jeff Campbell, has donated nearly 8,000 instruments in the last twenty-one years and impacted many thousands more children. They have donated musical instruments in forty-five states and twelve countries in the organization's history.

One child, whose story demonstrates Hungry for Music's tremendous impact, is that of Nora, who received a violin from Hungry for Music over a decade ago when she was living in an orphanage in Magdalena, Mexico. She grew up to not only play, but also to teach. Hungry for Music recently donated more instruments to Nora so she can teach her students. She said the instrument she received as a young girl changed her life, and she, in turn, wants to use music to change the lives of others.

How you can get involved

- Purchase CDs and t-shirts at the Hungry for Music Store
- Donate an instrument
- Donate funds directly to Hungry for Music

Scan to Learn More

or visit
www. hungryformusic.org

Read community stories
Donate
Get involved

About Music & Memory

MUSIC & MEMORY℠ is a nonprofit organization that brings personalized music into the lives of the elderly or infirm using digital music technology, vastly improving quality of life. They train elder care professionals in nursing homes and other settings, as well as family caregivers, how to create and provide personalized playlists using iPods, enabling those struggling with Alzheimer's, dementia, and other cognitive and physical challenges, to reconnect with the world through music-triggered memories.

By providing access and education, and by creating a network of MUSIC & MEMORY℠ Certified Care Organizations, Music & Memory aims to make this form of personalized therapeutic music a standard of health care.

The astonishing results of Music & Memory's program are documented in *Alive Inside*, a film by Michael Rossato-Bennett that follows Music & Memory founder Dan Cohen on his journey to bring music to those in need. This uplifting film chronicles the stories of multiple individuals around the United States and Canada who have experienced the healing power of music through the MUSIC & MEMORY℠ Program, including the story of Henry who suffered from dementia for a decade and would barely speak until Music & Memory set up an iPod program at his nursing home. *Alive Inside* was the winner of the 2014 Sundance Film Festival Audience Award for US Documentary. Scan the QR code below to watch Henry's story, order *Alive Inside*, donate, or get involved with Music & Memory.

How you can get involved

- Become a volunteer to help raise awareness
- Host an iPod donation drive
- Give an iPod
- Bring MUSIC & MEMORY℠ Certification to your care organization
- Donate funds directly to Music & Memory

Scan to Learn More
or visit
www. musicandmemory.org

Watch Henry's story
Order *Alive Inside*
Donate and get involved

Acknowlegments

There are several people who helped bring *Stories of Music* to life, and I am forever grateful for each of them. The contributing authors and artists, and their fascinating stories, helped me to compile an anthology beyond my expectations. They shared in my excitement for the project and offered incredible support throughout the process of publication.

Dan Cohen and Justin Russo at Music & Memory and Jeff Campbell at Hungry for Music also provided amazing support as I worked to incorporate the stories of their organizations into this book. Their service to bring music into people's lives continues to be an inspiration to me; it has been an honor to work with each of them.

Stories of Music would continue to be an idea for "someday" without the overwhelming encouragement of my husband, R.J. Nashleanas, who gave me the opportunity to make this a reality, and who managed the technology for the project. I am appreciative that he shares my passion for music, creativity, and giving back to the community. I couldn't ask for a better partner in this venture, and in life as a whole.

I owe many thanks to my parents, Wendy and Bob Tripp, who believed in this project every step of the way and offered both business and financial support. Music has been integral in our family history—from where this concept derived—and it bonds us still.

Kim Retzlaff, a dear friend and editor extraordinaire, was a priceless resource to me as I worked through editing the stories. Amy Wright, a friend of nearly twenty years, who also happens to be a talented marketer, helped me to promote this book from the start. I am indebted to both Kim and Amy for their expert advice and time on the project, and I hope they are proud of *Stories of Music* in its final form.

Thanks also to Kevin Walter, who contributed to implementing the technology needed for the web edition, and Gary Beswick who helped me arrive at the Yudu publishing platform for both the web edition and the app. And thank you to Frank Partipilo at Frederic Printing for putting so much consideration into fulfilling my vision of the print book.

I am very fortunate to have a strong network of family, friends, and colleagues who helped me to create *Stories of Music*. The collective support of everyone has been invaluable.

-Holly E. Tripp

References

"A Short Walk Through Music's Long History: Musicians on foot, past and present"

Chaytor, H.J., 1912. *The Troubadours*. Cambridge University Press, New York.

Cohen, D. & Greenwood, B., 1981. *The Buskers: A History of Street Entertainment*. David & Charles Inc., North Pomfret, Vt.

Cohoon, J.W., 1939. *Dio Chrysostom: Discourses 12-30*. Loeb Classical Library, Cambridge.

Frank, R., 1993. The Search for the Anglo-Saxon Oral Poet. *Bulletin of the John Rylands University Library of Manchester*, 75:11.

Gaunt, S. & Kay, S., editors, 1999. *The Troubadours: An Introduction*. Cambridge University Press, New York.

Jas Obrecht Music Archive, 2011. Johnny Shines: The Complete 1989 Living Blues Interview. http://jasobrecht.com/johnny-shines-complete-living-blues-interview/ (accessed Sept. 20, 2015).

Lewis-Williams, J.D., 2002. *The Mind in the Cave: Consciousness and the Origins of Art*. Thames & Hudson, New York.

Meayhew, H., 1851. *London Labour and the London Poor* (R. O'Day & D. Englander, editors). Wordsworth Editions Ltd., Hertfordshire, U.K.

Morley, I. *The Evolutionary Origins and Archaeology of Music*. Doctoral dissertation. Cambridge University, Cambridge, U.K., 2003.

Palmer, R., 1982. *Deep Blues: A Musical and Cultural History of the Mississippi Delta*. Penguin Books Ltd., Harmondsworth, Middlesex, England.

Reznikoff, I. & Dauvois, M., 1988. La Dimension Sonore des Grottes Ornées [article in French]. *Bulletin de la Société Préhistorique Française*, 85:8:238.

Sullivan, M., 2001. African-American Music as Rebellion: From Slavesong to Hip Hop. *Discoveries*, 3:21.

Trehub, S.E.; Becker, J.; & Morley, I., 2015. Cross-Cultural Perspective on Music and Musicality. *Philosophical Transactions B*, 370:1664.

Widsith, in the Exeter Book. Alexander, M., 1977. *The Earliest English Poems*. Penguin, London.

About the Contributors

(in alphabetical order)

ATA MOHAMMAD ADNAN is a doctor by profession, and a photographer out of passion. He is a street photographer who loves to photograph people around his hometown in Chittagong, Bangladesh, and in all the places he travels with his beloved camera. He has won national and international awards including 1st Place, Bangladesh in the National Awards as part of the 2015 Sony World Photography Awards. Follow Adnan's work at www.facebook.com/aadnansphotography.

ANNA ALFEROVA is a Moscow-based photographer whose work is often inspired by music and has been featured in several local exhibits. She graduated from Moscow State University where she studied the history of photography. Learn more about her work at www.alferovaphotography.com.

BENJAMIN ALLMON is an Australia-based freelance journalist and professional musician with a monthly music-related column, "Lyricbuster," in *Punchnel's Magazine*. His debut book, *Foot Notes*, is a chronicle of his 600-mile trek to promote his 2006 album, and is due out through Odyssey Books mid 2016. A certified audio engineer of twenty years, a member of the ASA, APRA, TAXI, and the QWC, Allmon is a graduate of the Morris Journalism Academy. In his spare time, he pens songs about pigs so that his three-year-old son can make oinking noises.

CRAIG BAKER is a Tucson-based writer whose work has appeared in various local publications including *The DesertLeaf*, *Tucson Weekly*, and *Zócalo Magazine*, as well as in national forums like Movoto.com and MentalFloss.com. Baker also works in public relations and dabbles in fiction from his home office.

CHINMOY BISWAS is a school teacher by profession, but is also passionate about photography through which he captures nature and people. Based in India, Biswas regularly participates in photography salons and competitions. He has won numerous awards both nationally and internationally, including the Salon International Photo-phylles (France) 2014 UPI Silver medal and the Sille Sanat Sarayi International Salon (Turkey) FIAP Gold medal in 2015.

KARINA BOROWICZ is the author of *Proof* (2014), winner of the Codhill Poetry Award. Her début poetry volume, *The Bees Are Waiting* (2012), won the Marick Press Poetry Prize and the Eric Hoffer Award, and it was named a Must Read by the Massachusetts Center for the Book.

BRUT CARNIOLLUS is a visual artist and photographer from Slovenia who creates photographic digital collages executed as original large format digital UV prints. His work is exhibited and awarded worldwide. See more of his work at www.carniollus.com.

BILL CUSHING has published poems in *Avocet*, *Brownstone Review*, *Penumbra*, *genius & madness*, the *Onion River Review*, the *Synergist*, *Spectrum*, and the *Sabal Palm Review*. Cushing teaches English classes at both Mount San Antonio and East Los Angeles colleges.

BHASKAR DAS is a surgeon by profession and an award-winning photographer based in Chandannagar, India. His work has earned him the Gold Medal-Portrait in the Egypt International Photo Contest in 2014, honorable mention for his photo story, "Circus" as part of IPA's Lucie Awards in 2012, and inclusion in the best 50 images in Shoot the Frame's "Shoot the Face" contest in 2014. His photography has also been published in *BLUR Magazine*, and more than 200 of his works have been accepted in national and international salons of photography.

ALLAND DHARMAWAN is an award-winning photographer from Indonesia whose work has been published by UNESCO Bangkok, Voice of America, WEXAS Travel, *Bangkok Post*, *The Nation*, *Thousand Islands Daily*, *Radar Malang*, and *Radar Jember*. He has explored the genres of portrait, landscape, food, macro, and culture photography, and has exhibited in Indonesia as well as internationally. In 2012, he participated in the "Indonesia" photo exhibition in Jakarta, which was exclusive for the President and the Ministers of the Republic of Indonesia. In 2013, his works were exhibited at Bangkok Art & Cultural Center in Thailand and at Penrith Regional Gallery & The Lewers Bequest in Australia. In 2014, his work won the Jury Prize from the 36th FIAP Youth Print Biennial (Germany). Follow Dharmawan on Instagram at @allanddharmawan and allanddharmawan.com.

ANNETTE DI GIOSIA became a member of the cello section of the San Antonio Symphony in the fall of 1966. She soon married her stand partner, Giovanni, and the two shared their gifts and talents with the San Antonio Symphony for forty-seven years. They also played Principal and Assistant Principal with the San Antonio Opera. While her husband passed away in 2013, Di Giosia continues to play and share her gift by teaching and playing with the Symphony of the Hills and the Mid-Texas Symphony.

DARRIN DUFORD has written for the *San Francisco Chronicle*, BBC Travel, *Gastronomica*, *Roads & Kingdoms*, PerceptiveTravel.com, and *Transitions Abroad*, among others. His work was recently anthologized in *Adventures of a Lifetime: Travel Tales from Around the World*, released in January 2015 by World Traveler Press. Follow him on Twitter at @darrinduford.

MARIA EDIBLE is a writer and photographer currently living in Jersey City, New Jersey. She is a retired competitive eater and a former tattoo model. Her work has been published in the *New York Post*, *Narratively*, *Zombie Guide Magazine*, and *Flash Fiction Magazine*. Find her on Instagram at @maria_edible and on Twitter at @mariaedible.

PATRICIA J. ESPOSITO is author of *Beside the Darker Shore* and has published numerous works in anthologies and magazines, including Main Street Rag's *Crossing Lines*, Annapurna's *Clarify*, *Scarlet Literary Magazine*, *Rose and Thorn*, *Karamu*, *Not One of Us*, and *Midnight Street*, with work forthcoming in Cohesion Press's *Blurring the Lines*. Esposito has received honorable mentions in "year's best" collections and is a Pushcart Prize nominee.

PETER GERSTENZANG is a humorist and freelance journalist who writes about dogs and popular culture, particularly music and film. He is a frequent blogger for *Rolling Stone*, the *Village Voice*, *The Huffington Post*, and other sites. He also directs music videos and recently completed his fourth video, "Another Sun is Setting" for the band Sad About Girls. Gerstenzang graduated from Columbia University with a bachelor's degree and a master's degree in fine arts.

STEVE GIVENS is a writer of children's books, journalism, poetry, songs, and spiritual essays. A long-time university administrator, he currently serves as associate vice chancellor and chief of staff in the Office of the Chancellor at Washington University in St. Louis, Missouri. As a composer, performer, and writer, his words and music have been used in concert, on stage, and in many video and audio productions, including two Emmy Award-winning PBS documentaries on the Gateway Arch and the 1904 St. Louis World's Fair. His current music collaborations are with the Mo Bottom Project, which seeks to capture the history, landscape, and spirit of the St. Louis-area Mississippi and Missouri River valleys. Two of his children's books, *The Violin Lesson and the Cross Street Band* (New Canaan Publishing) and *A Dream That Pulls You Through* (unpublished) carry themes of the healing and community-building power of music.

NANCY GUSTAFSON has published poetry, short fiction, and memoirs. She lives with her husband, Jan, in Huntsville, Texas. She may be found in the kitchen, the garden, at the sewing machine or, most often, writing at her desk.

KEN HAMBERG composes and produces music, and writes reviews and editorial content for the web out of the home he shares with his wife, teenaged son, and bizarre canine creature in New York City. A professional musician for more than 35 years, his recent output includes music for television and radio spots, scores for industrial videos, and some high-profile dance remixes with the legendary DJ/producer, Mark Kamins. For more information about Surrender, visit the band's website at www.surrendertunes.com.

EVELYN HAMPTON grew up on a farm in Colts Neck and in rural Tinton Falls, New Jersey, where she acquired a great appreciation and reverence for the peaceful beauty of nature and the comfort of small-town living in an era of bygone simplicity. She is inspired to take pen to paper by everyday living and the restorative power of music, poetry, and human connections. Hampton has published poems and essays in the *Monmouth Review*, and participated in the Long Branch Poetry Festival. She has served as a featured reader and conducted poetry workshops for the Monmouth County public library system.

KAREN PAUL HOLMES has a master's degree in Music History from the University of Michigan and has taught music appreciation at the college level. She's now a freelance writer and poet. She authored a full-length poetry collection, *Untying the Knot* (Aldrich Press, 2014), and her other publishing credits include *Poetry East, Atlanta Review, Town Creek Poetry, The Sow's Ear Poetry Review*, and *The Southern Poetry Anthology Volume V: Georgia* (Texas Review Press). Holmes received an Elizabeth George Foundation grant for poetry. To support fellow writers, she originated and hosts a critique group in Atlanta and Writers' Night Out in the Blue Ridge Mountains.

ROBERT WILLIAM IVENIUK is a Toronto-based author, screenwriter, and columnist. His short-fiction has been featured in *Schlock Magazine*, two volumes of *The Alchemy Press Book of Pulp Heroes* anthologies, and the *Long Hidden* anthology published by Crossed Genres Publications. His nonfiction articles have been featured on BlogTO and in *Archenemy Magazine* and *Urban Fantasy Magazine*.

ALEKSANDR KUZNETCOV is a professional musician from Russia who graduated from the St. Petersburg Conservatory. In addition to his passion for music he also enjoys photography, particularly photographing other musicians because he understands them very well. Through his photography, Kuznetcov tries to reflect the internal state of his subjects.

LAPIS is the result of worlds colliding and heading together in a new direction. Pushing the edge of cultural hybridity, their sound is informed by the traditional music of South Asia, Dub, Hip Hop, and Electronic Music. Lapis is composed of sitarist Mohamed Assani, vocalist and electronic musician, Rup Sidhu, and percussionist, Curtis Andrews. They are known for their love of improvisation and original compositions with unexpected sonic pairings such as wave drums and sitars, freestyle rap and mridangam, mbira, and beat boxing.

Having been classically trained in both Western and Hindustani music, Assani brings unique compositions and a sophisticated melodic sensibility to the group. Sidhu releases raw expression and refined aesthetics through electronics, beat boxing, and rapping. To round out the sounds of Lapis, Andrews shares his dynamic grooves and rhythms from South India and West Africa. Think of them like a 7-layer dip of intercontinental music—you never know what you'll get next but you just keep reaching for more. Lapis is based in Vancouver, Coast Salish Territories.

RICHARD LEBLOND is a retired biologist living in North Carolina. He has been writing about life experiences, travel to Europe and North Africa in the 1970s, and more recent adventures in eastern Canada and the US West. His essays and photographs have appeared in several US and international journals.

MARK MANDEVILLE & RAIANNE RICHARDS, who have been performing for over a decade, resonate with lovers of Americana, old country, and harmony singing, commanding crafted melodies and poignant, introspective lyrics, backing them with delicate arrangements on ukulele, clarinet, penny whistle, guitar, and banjo. They are respected for an authentic, heartfelt approach to their craft by audiences across the eastern US. Fred Knittel of WXPN in Philadelphia noted, "The best part of their performance is the undeniable chemistry Mark and Raianne have together; they play with a comfortability and trust that can only come with years of partnership. They allow enough space in their musical bond for us to settle in and witness some serious songwriting and playing." Learn more about Mandeville and Richards at www.markmandeville.com.

In addition to writing and performing, Mandeville and Richards founded an organization called The Massachusetts Walking Tour, which functions as a nonprofit to support arts and culture in the small towns of their home state. Each summer since 2010, a string of concerts are arranged in collaboration with local arts councils, school systems, town parks and recreation, and a variety of cultural groups to highlight the town's respective commitment to the arts. Mandeville, Richards, and chosen bands of talented folks from the northeast walk, laden with heavy packs and instruments, to each concert where they perform a folk music program alongside local artists, poets, and musicians. Learn more at www.masswalkingtour.org.

JERIN MICHEAL is a press and editorial photographer currently studying at Falmouth University in the South West Coast of England. At age eighteen, he has already won the prestigious NME's Under 18 Music Photographer of the Year and he has also exhibited his work at the Louvre in Paris. His subjects vary from world renowned musicians to deep-sea fishermen. No matter what he turns his lens to, he is enthralled by the story. When he isn't shooting, he enjoys good coffee and bad films. See more of Micheal's work at www.jerinmichealphotography.com.

BEN MURRAY is an Alberta-based writer, car-free vegan, and occasional sax player/drummer whose debut volume of poetry, *What We're Left With*, was published by Brindle & Glass. His idols include Keith Jarrett, Dexter Gordon, Miles Davis, Paul Watson, Woody Allen, P.K. Page, and Ian McEwan. Way back in the day, Murray once traded fours with Lew Tabackin, but is pretty sure Tabackin got the raw end of that particular trade! His fiction and poetry has been published in many journals and periodicals, and he was long-listed for the 2011 Best Canadian Poetry in English and the CBC Canada Writes 2012 Creative Non-Fiction Prize. He won the 2011 Jerry Jazz Short-Fiction Prize.

TRACIE RENEE AMIRANTE PADAL is a librarian at a busy public library in suburban Chicago, and she knows firsthand that words and music can bring people together, open doors to hope, and enrich the soul. A former teen music critic at the *Daily Herald* newspaper, Tracie's short stories and poems have won contests (sponsored by Scholastic, *Seventeen*, *USA Weekend*, Xerox/DocuWorld, the Northwest Cultural Council, Highland Park Poetry, and the Tallgrass Writers Guild) and have been published in magazines (*The Bark*), anthologies (*In Our Own Words: a Generation Defining Itself* and *Embers and Flames*), and literary journals (*Apocalypse*, *The Claremont Review*, *JUMP*, *The Louisville Review*, *Moon Journal*, and the *Oyez Review*). Most recently, Padal earned Featured Reader status at the 2015 Printers Row Lit Fest in Chicago and also headlined a reading at Powell's Bookstore. She has been nominated for the Pushcart Prize.

AARON PARRETT is a writer, musician, and teacher in Montana. He has written various essays and a dozen short stories that have appeared in places like *The Massachusetts Review*, *Open Spaces*, *Wild Blue Yonder*, *The Wisconsin Review*, and *Janus Head*. You can also read some of his latest work in his book, *LITERARY BUTTE: A History in Novels and Film*. Learn more about Parrett at www.aaronparrett.org.

JULIA PRICE is a flutist, composer, and electric sound designer who develops her craft through a sound lens of jazz, classical, world, electronic, improvisation, science, philosophy, and multi-medium collaboration. Based in North Carolina, she has performed and collaborated with Reggie Workman, Andrea E. Woods Valdés, *Voices—Chapel Hill*, Code f.a.d. Company, David Boykin, the Joe Robinson Quintet, Greg Osby, Nicole Mitchell, and many other artists, musicians, collectives, peers, and professionals. Learn more about Price at www.juliaprice.org.

VINESH RAJPAUL is a PhD student at the University of Oxford. While he researches astrophysics, he is also a passionate (obsessive) photographer. He grew up in Cape Town, South Africa, a city he considers to be the most beautiful in the world; and he also enjoys the beauty of Oxford: both cities are paradises for a photographer! Rajpaul's other life passion is music—he plays the piano, has found solace in music, and met his now wife at a piano recital in Oxford.

DEBRA RAVER is a singer-songwriter and former US Fulbright fellow to Lithuania. She earned an MA in ethnomusicology from Indiana University in 2014, where she furthered her childhood dream to "write all about Lithuania someday" and the musical legacy of her mother's homeland. Raver recently purchased a creative arts studio in Wyoming, her native state, to seed her next song and story project.

STEPHANIE REITANO is a writer, poet, artist, and lover of music. Her poetry has been featured in several anthologies throughout the years. Currently, Stephanie is a freelance writer, who also publishes poetry online at www.hellopoetry.com under the pen name PrttyBrd.

DAVID ROBERTS is a photographer and teacher based in Yorkshire, England. At university, he studied traditional film-based photography. Though having embraced digital techniques, his heart is still in the darkroom! He has a passion for travel photography and images from his travels have been featured in *The Guardian*, *The Independent*, and *The Telegraph* newspapers. Follow David's work at www.facebook.com/moonstonephotographic and www.moonstonephotographic.com.

RUTH SABATH ROSENTHAL is a New York poet, well published in literary journals and poetry anthologies throughout the US, and also internationally. In October 2006, her poem "on yet another birthday" was nominated for a Pushcart prize. She has five books of poetry available for purchase on Amazon.com: *Facing Home* (a chapbook); *Facing Home and Beyond*; *little, but by no means small*; *Gone, but Not Easily Forgotten*; and *Food: Nature vs. Nurture*. Learn more about her work at www.newyorkcitypoet.com.

KENNETH SALZMANN is a writer and poet whose work has appeared in numerous newspapers, magazines, and literary journals, as well as such anthologies as *Child of My Child: Poems and Stories for Grandparents* (Gelles-Cole Literary Enterprises), a Finalist (Anthology) in the 2011 Next Generation Indie Book Awards; *Beloved on the Earth: 150 Poems of Grief and Gratitude* (Holy Cow! Press); *Riverine: An Anthology of Hudson Valley Writers* (Codhill Press); and *The Heart of All That Is: Reflections on Home* (Holy Cow! Press). He lives in Woodstock, New York, and Ajijic, Mexico, with his wife, editor Sandi Gelles-Cole. Learn more about Salzmann at www.kensalzmann.com.

AMANDA SCHREIER is a Maryland-based freelance culture and travel writer who can't help but wander into small towns, war zones, diners, and haunted insane asylums. She has a master's degree in journalism and international affairs from Columbia University. Follow Schreier on Twitter at @BackroadsRamblr.

BAR SCOTT is a singer, songwriter, and writer who has recorded seven albums of original songs, and has published one book. Scott engineers, records, and edits most of her vocals and piano in her home studio, but leans on Dave Cook for the heavy studio lifting. Some of her favorite gigs have been in living rooms, but she has also sung at St. John the Divine Cathedral in New York City, Tarrytown Music Hall, Saturday Night Ramble with Levon Helm, the Beacon Theater with Phoebe Snow and Beth Nielsen Chapman, and one of the most powerful, in the pit at Ground Zero with Delores Holmes. Scott and Holmes (of Springsteen fame) sang Scott's "Grace" with Holmes's sisters for rescue workers who only days before had finished their difficult work there. Scott spent most of her professional life in Woodstock, New York, and now resides in rural Colorado. Learn more about Scott at www.barscott.com.

LYNN L. SHATTUCK is a columnist for the elephant journal and mom.me. Her work has also appeared in *Brain, Child*; *The Mid*; *Scary Mommy*; and *Purple Clover*; and two recently published anthologies, *Clash of the Couples* and *SMITH: Surviving Mental Illness Through Humor*. Shattuck blogs at www.thelightwillfindyou.com.

NOLAN STEVENS is a South African, award-winning artist, and a freelance journalist who has written for publications such as *One Small Seed Magazine*, jhblive.com, and *FUNK Magazine*, to name a few. His art has been a part of numerous group exhibitions, the highlight of which being the "South African Voices–A New Generation of Printmakers" group exhibition held at Washington DC's Washington Print Gallery.

HEIDI SWEDBERG has been making connections through music—between cultures and generations—for the past fifteen years. She lives in Los Angeles and teaches and plays an instrument that makes people smile: a ukulele. Twenty years working as an actor in the entertainment industry (a few seasons in the cast of *Seinfeld* was her most notable gig) led Swedberg to the realization that those two things, entertainment and industry, were antithetical to what she wanted to do—engagement and empowerment were lacking. The gift of children helped her find her path of meaningful work, and she now teaches and performs for all ages on small stages. Learn more about Swedberg's music at www.sukeyjumpmusic.com.

JARI THYMIAN has written poetry that has appeared in a variety of publications including *Matrix*, *Ekphrasis*, *Ken*Again*, *Memoir (and)*, *The Pedestal Magazine*, *The Christian Science Monitor*, *FRiGG*, *Alehouse*, *Pirene's Fountain*, *Margie*, *Flutter Poetry Journal*, *Prune Juice*, *Journal of Compressed Creative Arts*, and *American Tanka*. Thymian's poetry has been nominated for Best of the Net and a Pushcart Prize. Her chapbook, *The Meaning of Barns*, was published by Finishing Line Press.

JAMIE VIROSTKO is a storyteller, writer, and theatre artist based in Venice, California. Her original play, *The Outskirts of Paradise*, received its world premiere in LA in 2007. More recently Virostko published a collection of her favorite personal stories entitled, *Tiny Sagas of a Former Girl Scout*.

ANNA WALL is an art teacher for elementary students and loves inspiring children to use their artistic talents as a way to express themselves and learn coping skills. She is also a philanthropist who helps her daughter raise money for Children's Hospital Colorado through their nonprofit, Art by Adelyn, and is helping her other daughter start a nonprofit for dance scholarships. She previously worked in the publishing industry, and as a research assistant for a group of scientists at NIST and NASA, helping them prepare their research for publication. Wall graduated from the University of Colorado Boulder with a bachelor of science degree in journalism and a minor in psychology. She resides in Denver, Colorado with her husband and three children, ages nine, seven, and four.

CARLO ZAMORA is a photographer and operations manager of an import/export company in the Philippines. His photography has won many awards including 3rd Place, Philippines National Award, Sony World Photography Awards (2014); 1st Place Portrait Photographer of the Year at Maybank Photo Awards in Malaysia (2013); 2nd Place Portrait Photographer of the Year from Imaging Resources (2008); and 2nd Place *Digital Camera World* Portrait Photographer of the Year (2007).

VINESH RAJPAUL is a PhD student at the University of Oxford. While he researches astrophysics, he is also a passionate (obsessive) photographer. He grew up in Cape Town, South Africa, a city he considers to be the most beautiful in the world; and he also enjoys the beauty of Oxford: both cities are paradises for a photographer! Rajpaul's other life passion is music—he plays the piano, has found solace in music, and met his now wife at a piano recital in Oxford.

DEBRA RAVER is a singer-songwriter and former US Fulbright fellow to Lithuania. She earned an MA in ethnomusicology from Indiana University in 2014, where she furthered her childhood dream to "write all about Lithuania someday" and the musical legacy of her mother's homeland. Raver recently purchased a creative arts studio in Wyoming, her native state, to seed her next song and story project.

STEPHANIE REITANO is a writer, poet, artist, and lover of music. Her poetry has been featured in several anthologies throughout the years. Currently, Stephanie is a freelance writer, who also publishes poetry online at www.hellopoetry.com under the pen name PrttyBrd.

DAVID ROBERTS is a photographer and teacher based in Yorkshire, England. At university, he studied traditional film-based photography. Though having embraced digital techniques, his heart is still in the darkroom! He has a passion for travel photography and images from his travels have been featured in *The Guardian*, *The Independent*, and *The Telegraph* newspapers. Follow David's work at www.facebook.com/moonstonephotographic and www.moonstonephotographic.com.

RUTH SABATH ROSENTHAL is a New York poet, well published in literary journals and poetry anthologies throughout the US, and also internationally. In October 2006, her poem "on yet another birthday" was nominated for a Pushcart prize. She has five books of poetry available for purchase on Amazon.com: *Facing Home* (a chapbook); *Facing Home and Beyond*; *little, but by no means small*; *Gone, but Not Easily Forgotten*; and *Food: Nature vs. Nurture*. Learn more about her work at www.newyorkcitypoet.com.

KENNETH SALZMANN is a writer and poet whose work has appeared in numerous newspapers, magazines, and literary journals, as well as such anthologies as *Child of My Child: Poems and Stories for Grandparents* (Gelles-Cole Literary Enterprises), a Finalist (Anthology) in the 2011 Next Generation Indie Book Awards; *Beloved on the Earth: 150 Poems of Grief and Gratitude* (Holy Cow! Press); *Riverine: An Anthology of Hudson Valley Writers* (Codhill Press); and *The Heart of All That Is: Reflections on Home* (Holy Cow! Press). He lives in Woodstock, New York, and Ajijic, Mexico, with his wife, editor Sandi Gelles-Cole. Learn more about Salzmann at www.kensalzmann.com.

AMANDA SCHREIER is a Maryland-based freelance culture and travel writer who can't help but wander into small towns, war zones, diners, and haunted insane asylums. She has a master's degree in journalism and international affairs from Columbia University. Follow Schreier on Twitter at @BackroadsRamblr.

BAR SCOTT is a singer, songwriter, and writer who has recorded seven albums of original songs, and has published one book. Scott engineers, records, and edits most of her vocals and piano in her home studio, but leans on Dave Cook for the heavy studio lifting. Some of her favorite gigs have been in living rooms, but she has also sung at St. John the Divine Cathedral in New York City, Tarrytown Music Hall, Saturday Night Ramble with Levon Helm, the Beacon Theater with Phoebe Snow and Beth Nielsen Chapman, and one of the most powerful, in the pit at Ground Zero with Delores Holmes. Scott and Holmes (of Springsteen fame) sang Scott's "Grace" with Holmes's sisters for rescue workers who only days before had finished their difficult work there. Scott spent most of her professional life in Woodstock, New York, and now resides in rural Colorado. Learn more about Scott at www.barscott.com.

LYNN L. SHATTUCK is a columnist for the elephant journal and mom.me. Her work has also appeared in *Brain, Child*; *The Mid*; *Scary Mommy*; and *Purple Clover*; and two recently published anthologies, *Clash of the Couples* and *SMITH: Surviving Mental Illness Through Humor*. Shattuck blogs at www.thelightwillfindyou.com.

NOLAN STEVENS is a South African, award-winning artist, and a freelance journalist who has written for publications such as *One Small Seed Magazine*, jhblive.com, and *FUNK Magazine*, to name a few. His art has been a part of numerous group exhibitions, the highlight of which being the "South African Voices–A New Generation of Printmakers" group exhibition held at Washington DC's Washington Print Gallery.

HEIDI SWEDBERG has been making connections through music—between cultures and generations—for the past fifteen years. She lives in Los Angeles and teaches and plays an instrument that makes people smile: a ukulele. Twenty years working as an actor in the entertainment industry (a few seasons in the cast of *Seinfeld* was her most notable gig) led Swedberg to the realization that those two things, entertainment and industry, were antithetical to what she wanted to do—engagement and empowerment were lacking. The gift of children helped her find her path of meaningful work, and she now teaches and performs for all ages on small stages. Learn more about Swedberg's music at www.sukeyjumpmusic.com.

JARI THYMIAN has written poetry that has appeared in a variety of publications including *Matrix*, *Ekphrasis*, *Ken*Again*, *Memoir (and)*, *The Pedestal Magazine*, *The Christian Science Monitor*, *FRiGG*, *Alehouse*, *Pirene's Fountain*, *Margie*, *Flutter Poetry Journal*, *Prune Juice*, *Journal of Compressed Creative Arts*, and *American Tanka*. Thymian's poetry has been nominated for Best of the Net and a Pushcart Prize. Her chapbook, *The Meaning of Barns*, was published by Finishing Line Press.

JAMIE VIROSTKO is a storyteller, writer, and theatre artist based in Venice, California. Her original play, *The Outskirts of Paradise*, received its world premiere in LA in 2007. More recently Virostko published a collection of her favorite personal stories entitled, *Tiny Sagas of a Former Girl Scout*.

ANNA WALL is an art teacher for elementary students and loves inspiring children to use their artistic talents as a way to express themselves and learn coping skills. She is also a philanthropist who helps her daughter raise

Submit your story about music
to be considered for publication
in a future volume.

www.storiesofmusic.com

CPSIA information can be obtained
at www.ICGtesting.com
Printed in the USA
LVOW05s1819180216
475696LV00037B/161/P